AUTHENTIC CONNECTION

AUTHENTIC CONNECTION

What You've Been Missing and How to Find It

Leah Marie Price

For Solomon

Table of Contents

Foreword

In the spring of 2022, I had a chance meeting with Leah. I had presented at a large conference in Nashville, Tennessee, with over 8,000 people in attendance. As you can imagine, finding a seat in the large plenary sessions at a conference of that size can be a challenge. I scanned the ballroom for available seats and asked a woman if the empty seat I'd spotted next to her was open. She gestured for me to sit and proceeded to tell me she had recently "met" me on a recorded video training she had reviewed as part of her work. It was so gratifying when she mentioned that the training I had done on the therapeutic alliance had helped her significantly improve her relationship with her 18-year-old son. I invited her to write the story she shared with me in an article for the upcoming installment of *Tips and Topics*, my monthly online publication.

We kept in touch throughout the process, and when Leah told me she was writing a book, I was impressed and then particularly interested in her topic of allowing ourselves to live joyfully as our authentic self. It aligned precisely because in my personal and professional life I, too, have been focused on that very journey. Now, as I reflect on holding the book in my hands, I marvel at the serendipity of that chance meeting and the mutual learning and growth it sparked.

It has been such a fun and informative process to read Leah's book, recognizing and remembering many of the stories that I was "with" her for as we talked over the real-time lessons learned from her life experiences. That is a part of the power of this book—the stories that give shape to the many effective tools and practices that allow you to be your authentic self.

As Leah candidly and vulnerably shares her journey to reconnecting with her authentic self, she speaks not from some removed academic philosophy. Through the lens of her personal journey, Leah skillfully distills both the science and her own experiential knowledge of trauma and heightens awareness of the self-imposed limitations that impede living proudly as the truest you. She guides the reader through the context and rationale for the practices and even expands the opportunities for knowledge and support through a variety of linked resources.

Leah displays talent and creativity in this first book. I thank Leah for including me in her unfolding life and career as a writer, teacher, and role model for walking the talk in the journey to allowing your Authentic Self. I am confident you will thank her too.

David Mee-Lee, M.D.

American Board of Addiction Medicine and Board-Certified Psychiatrist and Editor-in-Chief of the American Society of Addiction Medicine's (ASAM) Criteria (all editions from 1991 to 2013).

Introduction

"You've *got* to be kidding me," I uttered under my breath, not wanting to let my son hear the shock in my voice. "I should have read the topography map more closely ..."

He and I had just embarked on an adventure to hike our first "14-er," which is Colorado-speak for a mountain over 14,000 feet tall. On paper, Mt. Beirstadt seemed like it would be one of the least challenging 14-ers to climb. It was a well-worn trail and only about eight miles round trip to the summit and back. It was also not a climb that required ropes and gear and technical mountaineering experience; there would just be some rock scrambling near the top. The trail started at over 11,000 feet in elevation, too, so there was only about a 2,700-foot total elevation gain over four miles to get to the top.

The problem was, my brain had made the automatic assumption that the 2,700 feet of elevation gain would be fairly evenly distributed across the four miles, which would make it just a moderately steep climb. That sounded perfect for me because, frankly, I was a bit out of shape at the time. As soon as we set foot on the trail, I could see that I had been dead wrong about the elevation distribution. It was then that I realized, in dismay, what we were actually getting ourselves into.

As it turned out, the first quarter mile or so of the hike actually descended into a thick, boggy marshland, which we

3

would have to traverse for almost two miles before we even started the climb. What we thought was going to be a moderately challenging four-mile hike to the summit was actually going to be a two-mile, super easy, flat hike through the bog followed by a two-mile, basically vertical, ascent. Oh.

My son was twenty at the time and in the best shape of his life. If he'd wanted to, he probably could have run up the side of the mountain. I doubted the steepness of the hike would even faze him. For me, recently off the couch, however, I sensed that things were going to get difficult. I kept my dismay to myself, and we set off, descending into the marsh.

The marsh was eerie but intriguing. It seemed to go on forever. Finally, we started our ascent. After a brutal climb and some intense rock scrambling, it looked like we were almost at the top. I got really excited, but my excitement was short-lived. If you've ever climbed a mountain, you're familiar with the term "false summit." This is when you get to what you *thought* was the top of the mountain only to find that it's just the top of a smaller rise that is so steep that it is blocking your view of the *real* summit.

When we reached the false summit and I realized that we still had quite a ways to go, I stopped for a rest—my hands on my knees, bent over, breathing heavily. Part of me really wanted to just give up and face-plant in the dirt. My son could summit by himself and wake me up on his way back down.

Having that thought was how I knew the thin air was making me delirious. I wasn't giving up *now*! If I were to give up now, I would be passing up a once-in-a-lifetime opportunity I could never get back. I would be letting myself down and letting him down. We'd been talking about doing this hike together for a year. I then experienced a moment of intense and euphoric gratitude that the two of us were able to be on this hike at all. Considering some of the really tough things we'd been through in the years prior, it was honestly kind of a miracle that we were here, on an impossibly gorgeous, blue-skied summer day, about to summit a mountain together.

This felt like one of those defining moments in life where you either decide to blast through your discomfort, go the distance, and reach new heights, or quit, scurry back in your "safe" little hole, and spend the rest of your life trying to convince yourself that you're satisfied living in a hole.

Hell no. I hadn't come this far to stop now. And I was *never* going back in my hole. I stood up, wiped the sweat off my brow, and somehow summoned the energy to continue from somewhere deep inside. I started the final ascent, determined to keep putting one foot in front of the other.

As I plodded upward, navigating an immense field of boulders, it struck me that the unfolding of this hike bore a striking resemblance to the unfolding of my journey of reconnecting with my authentic self over the past few years.

When I had set out on *that* trail, I hadn't known that I would have to go down before I could go up, either. Denial works great, until it doesn't.

I hadn't anticipated a seemingly endless trek through a dark, marshy bog before I could start to climb up. That's how it is when we finally start exploring the pain we've spent our lives hiding from.

I also had *no idea* that the path of recovery would be so gruelingly steep. Turns out that trying to change a lifetime of fear-based conditioning, living in survival mode, and relying on unhealthy coping skills demands that one dig deep, accessing inner reserves of grit to keep going.

Your Inner Grit

If you picked up this book, I suspect you can relate to this struggle and to having a deep desire to journey home to your authentic self. Perhaps stress, anxiety, guilt, worry, fear, self-blaming, self-shaming, and unhealthy coping habits are robbing you of a happy life. Perhaps you're baffled by your patterns of self-sabotage and tired of feeling stuck all the time. Perhaps you're sick of feeling alone even when you're around other people, battling low self-confidence, and feeling unsatisfied in relationships. Perhaps you're tired of feeling "meh" all the time. Perhaps all of the above?

What would it mean to you to permanently overcome these struggles? What would it mean to you to finally get on with living your *real* life, the life you were *meant* to have, instead of spending another five years, ten years, twenty years, or more longing for it? This is what you deserve, my friend, and this is what you can have. So please, join me on this journey.

When we came into this world, each of us was a naturally loving, bright, curious, confident, playful, abundant, open, carefree soul. So quickly, that innate innocence and trust was conditioned out of us by our families, communities, and society. Sadly, this is the way things have been. Our parents were conditioned into fear and conformity by their parents, who were conditioned into fear and conformity by their parents, and so on, and so on, back into history for millennia.

Humans have always depended on one another for survival, originally in hunter-gatherer groups, and then in stationary communities, beginning with the dawn of agriculture. We are also a relationship-oriented species. We need relationships to survive and thrive. As Dr. Gabor Maté so eloquently describes in his book *The Myth of Normal*, because we need to be accepted in

I believe authentic connections are what we are missing, needing, and craving, in our personal and professional lives, and in society at large, and that the expansion in the number of people doing this work for themselves has the potential to effect massive healing. I know personally how powerfully healing authentic connections can be, so my motive is to do what I can to help others find relief from suffering and become empowered to be part of the solution, by developing authentic connections with themselves, others, and the natural world.

In this book, we will explore practices that you can employ to start your journey toward reconnecting with your authentic self. The practices I've outlined here are the practices that, over the years, have been instrumental in helping me reconnect with my authentic self. I hope that all I've learned along my own personal journey, along with my professional experience working in adult education, facilitation, and coaching with individuals and multi-disciplinary teams, can be leveraged to help others realize the importance and value of cultivating authentic connections with themselves and others—including those with our partners, our children, our wider families, our colleagues, our communities, and our environment.

The practices in each chapter build on the previous practices. I recommend reading them in order the first time through. After that, please feel free to engage with the practices in whatever ways inspire you to *apply* the information. Application is the most important part of the learning process. Absorbing concepts intellectually is the laying of the foundation. It is very necessary, but the bulk of learning happens experientially, by applying the concepts in real life and then evaluating both your methods and results. As you read, you will find I've interspersed stories, questions to stimulate contemplation, practical tools, and links to other resources that will hopefully help you successfully apply the principles in this book, so you may experience the immeasurable benefits of deepening your connection with your authentic, wonderful self.

The Mountaintop

I am happy to report that I was able to reach both of my mountaintops that day, the literal and the metaphorical. My son and I successfully summited Mt. Bierstadt together. We soaked in the warmth of the summer sun and took in the breathtaking views. Each of us felt a renewed sense of empowerment—that we could trust ourselves to go the distance for what was important to us. I believe this had a great impact on us both. For me personally, it was also a metaphorical summit—tangible proof that the personal journey I'd been on of healing from trauma, recovering from addiction, and reestablishing a strong connection with my authentic self, had been well worth the effort. That journey, too, had been a grueling climb, but it paid off in improved emotional, mental, and physical health and endurance that I am confident will help carry me further along the trail.

Learning to accept, love, trust, and express our authentic selves is the journey of a lifetime. It is a return to innocence, a great *unlearning* of all the societal programming that led us away from our authentic selves, which have always been alive in us, inextinguishable.

I hope that this book can be a supportive companion to you along your journey of unlearning the false beliefs and limitations that have caused you suffering, and learning how to reconnect with your authentic self. I would love to hear from you as you make your way, and I will be ever encouraging you in spirit!

1
Cultivate Awareness

"You are the universe in ecstatic motion.
Stop acting so small."
—Rumi

I was jolted awake by searing pain. It was the middle of the night. *Holy crap, this is it*, I thought. The moment I'd been awaiting for nine months. I was soon to become a mother. I shook my partner awake. "It's happening!"

As my words registered in his sleep-fogged brain, he jumped into action, rocketing out of bed to call our midwife, Mary Ann. He let her know that I'd fallen asleep with no signs of labor but had just woken up with intense contractions. Mary Ann was a well-seasoned midwife. She told him not to panic, that a first-time childbirth usually takes twelve to twenty-four hours, so he should just try to help me stay as comfortable as possible and call her back when the contractions were under two minutes apart.

Ten minutes later, they were coming in blinding waves about a minute and a half apart. "Get. MaryAnn. *Now*," I hissed between breaths. With eyes the size of dinner plates, my partner got up from my side without a word and ran back to the phone.

I don't remember hearing the details of their conversation. I just remember hearing his voice saying, "She's on her way!" from some distant place, as I was being swallowed by the next tsunami of pain. I had never encountered pain like that, nor have I since. Turns out women for millennia weren't lyin'. That shit *hurts*.

At the time, we were living about ten miles outside of Flagstaff, Arizona, in a little wooded village of homes near the top of a small mountain. Steep gravel roads wound their way around the mountainside up to our house. Mother Nature must have a real sense of humor because that night, of all nights, an unusually severe snow and ice storm swept across northern Arizona. This did not bode well for my midwife and her assistant getting to us speedily, if they were able to make it at all.

At this point, it may have seemed to an outsider that my decision to have a home birth was looking like a terrible idea. It was sort of looking like a terrible idea to *me*, if I'm being honest, but I did not allow myself to focus on my fear. Now was *not* the time to start freaking out. I knew I had one choice and one choice only: to stay the course, focus on things going *well*, and trust like I'd never trusted before.

One Bitch

While we may perceive ourselves as solid and separate from one another, we are really all clusters of energy and information, sharing space in the same energy and information soup that makes up all that exists. With an obscene degree of detail, each of us has been mysteriously, miraculously, and intelligently organized into an individual functioning, conscious organism.

When we drill down into matter though, past the molecule, past the atom, and even past the subatomic particles, what we perceive as solid matter is actually composed of what physicists call "energy packets," plurally referred to as "quanta," that behave like (hold your brain) *either* waves or particles, depending on the conditions they're exposed to. At our most fundamental energetic level, what we perceive as physical solidity is neither fixed *nor* solid, meaning physical solidity and individual separateness are actually subjective experiences, based on the sensory apparatus with which they are perceived. On an energetic level, we are each innately, inseparably connected to one another and everything that exists. Like the movie title, you could say, we're *Everything, Everywhere, All at Once*.

When we die, the clusters of energy and information that form the tissues of our bodies decay—or, to use a less graphic verb, *un-cluster*—slowly over time, back into the universal soup of molecules, atoms, subatomic particles, and waves of energy from whence they came. Like drops of rain falling back into the ocean, the energy that comprises each of our physical bodies and individual consciousnesses will one day disperse back into the whole of the quantum energy field. The energy that makes up "you" and "me" will not be gone; it will just be transmuted into whatever creation the intelligent organizing force of the universe has in store for it next.

We have many names for this primordial intelligent organizing force. God, Inner Being, Infinite Intelligence, Greater Awareness, Collective Consciousness, All That Exists, the Field, the Force ... I could go on, but the point is, whatever label each of us chooses to give it, we're all talking about the source of everything in existence, which could never be adequately described in words. To quote Albert Einstein, "My sense of God is my sense of wonder about the universe."

The Elasticity of Time

We all inherently know this. Think back on your life. Aren't there times that stick out in your memory when you felt that crystal clear, undeniable knowing that you were so much more than just a brain in a terminal bag of flesh? When you felt endless, unbound, and euphorically connected to everything?

Maybe you've fallen madly in love? Been "in the zone"? Been left rapt and speechless by a breathtaking sunset?

However one gets there, in these fleeting moments, the illusory veil between everyday perception and the field of eternal primordial intelligence drops away. We are momentarily free of the burdens of separation and linearity. There is an elasticity to our sense of time and a humming, full-body awareness of the life force that animates us.

For a few brief moments, our incessant mental chatter stops and we feel a crystalline clarity. We're not worrying about the past or projecting into the future. The *now* seems open and expansive. We are pure and innocent in our awareness, fully in the present moment, basking in its deliciousness. We are at one. Whole. Connected.

Fundamental Skills

Becoming aware of this oneness with the power that creates everything in existence also gives us the broader perspective we need to then explore *self*-awareness and its companion, metacognition. Self-awareness can be described as the ability to recognize and understand our own physical sensations, thoughts, emotions, and behaviors. In other words, it is the ability to detach from your singular perception of your personal reality and acknowledge that the personality you know as "you" is but one aspect of the collective consciousness in a physical body, with its own sensory apparatus with which to translate energy into information. Metacognition is defined as the "awareness and understanding of one's own thought processes." I like to think of it as the ability to think critically about your own thinking. Self-awareness and metacognition allow you to become the witness of yourself; to recognize and understand that you are a consciousness experiencing a body and that you are a consciousness experiencing a mind.

Practicing self-awareness and metacognition are acts of seeking to understand our own thought processes, emotions, bodies, and behaviors, for the ultimate purpose of gaining agency over them. We collect invaluable data as we learn to observe how our thoughts and focus impact our emotional and physical state, and start to notice what happens in our experience as a result. Self-awareness and metacognition are *fundamental* to learning how to get our fear-conditioned minds out of the way so we can put our authentic selves in the driver's seat.

With these two skills in hand, we can then begin to practice deliberately focusing our attention. Once we have developed the skill of focusing our attention at will, we will have opened the door to having immense creative power in our own lives; working from the inside out, turning our thoughts into reality, rather than just reacting to the environment as it comes at us. We will discuss this more in later chapters in this book.

You Don't Have to Wait to Cultivate

One of the best-kept secrets in life is that we don't have to sit around and wait for moments of greater awareness to spontaneously befall us. We don't have to be anything or do anything special to "earn" this feeling. We don't have to deprive ourselves in *this* life, crossing our fingers in the hope that there's an afterlife. We can practice feeling our attunement with the field of energy and intelligence, *here and now*, any time we choose to, by engaging in activities that allow us to come into the wondrous present moment and feel our oneness with the source of all that exists.

This is a process I like to call *cultivating awareness*. There are many productive mindfulness practices you might employ in order to cultivate awareness. The most powerful of them is meditation, which we'll talk about more in the next chapter. Other great tools for cultivating awareness include (but are not limited to) reflective writing, yoga, tai chi, qigong, deep breathing exercises, and engaging all of one's senses during any present moment activity (such as cooking, eating, bathing, walking, and the like). You can find a curated list of resources for cultivating greater awareness in your book bonuses at www.whyconnectionworks.com/bookbonuses, by navigating to the Authentic Connection Book Bonuses section. I encourage you to go explore and try on a few things to see which practices might be good fits for you.

The more I've consistently dedicated myself to cultivating awareness, the better my life has become. My relationships have become deeper, healthier, more loving, and more authentic. My career has taken off in a thrilling direction, which has helped my financial situation improve dramatically. I went spelunking into the darkest corners of my psyche, cleaning out ancient skeletons and cobwebs, which allowed me to ultimately recover from the addictions and post-traumatic stress disorder symptoms that were consuming me. I began to value myself enough to take better care of my health. As my joie de vivre has reignited, I've made room in my life to explore some of my long-shelved passions, such as dancing, writing, and photography. I have developed genuine confidence, self-trust, and self-respect. Instead of being riddled with anxiety and trying to escape my feelings at all costs, I finally feel truly present in my own life: exhilarated, peaceful, satisfied, supported, deeply connected, very free, and very alive.

I have no reservations in asserting that cultivating awareness is *the single most important thing you can do with your time. Period.* Viscerally experiencing your oneness with everything in existence is the only way to know fully who you really are and to understand your true power, in its breathtaking immensity.

Not a Moment Too Soon

I distinctly remember feeling the true magnitude of my existence and power when I held my newborn son in my arms for the first time. I swear, I could see the whole universe in his eyes. I was overflowing with awe. In that moment, I understood that I was but a conduit for this incredible life force, and my gratitude for the privilege of being able to create new life blew my heart wide open. There really aren't words to adequately describe the feeling.

So, as you've likely just deduced, my midwife and her assistant *did* make it to our house that icy cold winter's night, although barely in time! I went from a dead sleep to delivery in just four hours, which is pretty fast and furious, if you're familiar with the human birth process. It felt kind of like what I imagine being strapped to the front of a speeding freight train would feel like. I'm intensely glad that I trusted myself to know that it was time to get the midwife on her way when I did. Thankfully, there were no major complications.

I was definitely in awe of my body. What an incredible feat. I was also kind of in awe at the fact that I didn't let fear swallow me when things got dicey. I was somehow able to coach myself to hang on, trust my body, trust the process, and focus on the possibility of things working out well, despite the seemingly ominous odds. I was somehow able to surrender and commit to riding it out, come what may. I had no other choice, to be fair, but the body responds to the mind. Things could have turned out very differently had I let fear take over.

After his delivery, my son and I got to rest, recover, and bond in the comfort of our home for many days. It was an unforgettable slice out of time. I got to spend hours and hours just staring at his adorable little nose and fingers and toes. His cute, fluffy little eyelashes. The funny faces he made in his sleep! I had nothing to do but marvel at this tiny perfect little creation who taught me the most important thing I will ever learn in his first few breaths: *we are all connected and we are part of something bigger*.

Don't Knock It 'Til You Try It

I'm not asking you to believe that cultivating awareness will make a dramatic, positive impact in every area of your life just because I said so. I'm also not asking you to give birth to find out, unless you want to. I'm simply asking you to suspend any lingering *disbelief* you may have and engage in one or more of the aforementioned awareness-cultivating practices consistently for a few months, so you can gain the experiential knowledge you need to decide if this way of living is for you.

Maybe once you've given it a good try, you'll decide that having a permeating awareness of your oneness with others and the power that creates all of existence is just not your jam. If so, fair enough.

But maybe, just *maybe*, as you give it a try, you'll discover the unfathomable immensity and power of who you truly are. Maybe you'll discover that cultivating awareness has made a *dramatic, positive impact in every area of your life.*

2
Train Your Attention

"Attention is fundamentally the linkage between consciousness and any aspect of the world around us. Attention is what sets the stage for the choices and observations we make that force the cloud of infinite possibilities to become an actuality; to 'collapse the wave function,' in the parlance of quantum physics."
—Karen Newell

I don't know how I'm going to pull this off. I just know that I am.

That was the thought running through my head one memorable morning many years ago. I was in a division-wide meeting with a bunch of smart, successful, high-level professionals at the government agency I worked for.

Now, I'm no meeting enthusiast, but I was psyched to be in this particular meeting for one reason. It put me in close proximity to people from another team that I was dying to join. I had a strong passion for their mission and programs. I had no idea how I would wiggle my way into a spot on their team. I just knew it was *right* for me. When I thought of doing that work and having a real impact on justice reform, it gave me goose bumps.

As luck would have it, I had a chance to mingle with some of the people on that team while we all waited for the division director to call our meeting to order. We really hit it off. I remember feeling a tingle of excitement as I returned to my own team's table to sit down, and the director called the meeting to order.

Then, something strange happened. I was settling into the meeting, when, like tectonic plates shifting, something suddenly shifted in my perception. It almost felt like I was plunged underwater. My vision went blurry. I could hear that there were people talking, but their voices seemed muffled and distant. I was lost in a world of my own. Then, I experienced what felt like a spontaneous *download* of new information. Apparently, this is what the glorious surprise birth of a new idea feels like.

Just minutes prior, I had been feeling discouraged, seeing no avenue for me to get a position on that team, but suddenly I had this beautiful revelation that they really needed someone to develop a statewide training program for their specialized staff. I could be that person. The current training position I was in just happened to be the perfect place for me to acquire the skills I needed to get there. In a flash, it all made sense. A whole new world of possibilities I had not considered opened up before me. It was thrilling. For a few moments, I was fully at one with the possibility of my desire becoming reality, existing with it in a state of total potential and unfettered hope. It was kind of ecstatic.

Then, *of course*, the mental fuckery began.

My mind started telling me things like:

- "This position doesn't even exist. What? Are they going to just *create* a new position for you?! This is the government. Get real."

- "You just started the position you have *now*. They'll think you're full of yourself if you apply for another position too soon."
- "You barely even know these people. What makes you think they'd want to work with you, anyway?"
- "You don't have a master's degree. They *all* do. They'll think you're underqualified, and you probably are."
- "Why can't you just stay in your lane for once and be satisfied where you're at?"
- "Even if the position *did* exist, the competition would be fierce. You'd probably apply for it and not get it and then be more disappointed than ever."

Wow, right?! Even though I was aware of my fear-conditioned mind's propensity to try to talk me into staying small, I had to admit it was really going all out this time, doing the most to claw its way in and hijack this new desire. Probably because it was a great "big" desire with potentially career-catapulting prospects. That's usually how it works. The more of a big deal a desire feels like, the more the fear-conditioned mind starts trying to shut it down, tossing around all the reasons it's not likely to work out. This way, you don't risk venturing into unfamiliar territory. To the survival mechanisms of our nervous systems and our fear-conditioned minds, familiar equals safe, and unfamiliar equals dangerous. Even if the familiar is wildly uncomfortable, these parts of us still perceive the familiar as less scary than the unknown. You've already survived the familiar. You have not survived the unknown. Makes sense, but still. Uuuugggggghhhhh.

Then, I remembered that there was really only *one* factor that would determine the final outcome of this story. There was only one person who could stand between me and my shiny new desire, and that was *me*. The question was ...

Would I get out of my own way, or not?

What Will You Magnify?

Consider your attention to be the magnifying glass through which you view your reality. Like a hand can move a magnifying glass around, you are continually choosing where you place your attention, whether you do it consciously or unconsciously. Just like looking at anything through a magnifying glass, whatever you place your attention on becomes magnified in your perceptual experience. Put another way, whatever you place your attention on is what expands in your reality.

It is critical to note that, just like a magnifying glass magnifies whatever you point it at, the magnifying glass of your attention *also* does not exclude. To reiterate: it magnifies *whatever you point it at*, regardless of whether you want to see more of that thing or not. If you're focused on bad news, how broke you are, how stupid people are, and how getting old sucks, *that's* what you're magnifying in your experience. If you're focused on loving, having fun, enjoying life's abundance, and feeling good, *that's* what you're magnifying in your experience. Conceptually, it's really that simple. The challenging part is gaining *control* over where you point your magnifying glass.

Wield It Wisely

The quantum energy field we exist in is the field of all possibilities, the field of pure potential. Focusing your attention on something is how you "collapse the wave function" and "force the cloud of infinite possibilities to become an actuality." Put more simply, what you focus on is what you get.

Our nervous systems, including our brains, are continually taking in billions of sensory stimuli. As such, there is a constant, subconscious, automatic, survival-oriented filtering process happening that sorts out what sensory information is important for us to focus on and what sensory information is presently *not* as important for us to focus on. This is great. We love that this is happening without us having to work for it, so we can survive. The problem is, there is *so much* information coming at us all the time that our brains have to develop shortcuts to effectively perform this task. Additionally, we may have experienced trauma that left a deep impression on our nervous system, causing it to automatically and almost instantly flag certain stimuli as unsafe, if they are encountered again. These tendencies both naturally lead to categorizing and generalizing. That's fine when it's helpful for our survival. It's *not* ideal when it leads to knee-jerk reactions and biases that we may be unaware of but that negatively affect our behaviors, our quality of life, and the quality of life of those around us.

Your attention is a tool, just like a magnifying glass, and like all tools, with persistent daily training over time, you can become adept at deliberately using it. When we find ourselves focusing our attention on something we don't want to create more of, such as gridlock on the freeway, we can non-judgmentally choose to shift our attention to something we actually *do* want to magnify in our experience. Think of it like you're taking your attention to puppy obedience school. As soon as you notice that you're focusing your attention on a crappy thought you'd like to evict from your mental script, you can choose to lovingly redirect it to focus on something that aligns with empowering beliefs that serve you. Just like you would have to do with a puppy, you're going to have to do this over and over again, thought by thought, day by day, until your attention learns that you are in charge.

If you are the survivor of trauma in any form, especially developmental trauma in a dysfunctional family system or intimate relationship abuse, learning to take control of your attention and wield it wisely in service of your authentic self, versus letting your nervous system's survival mechanism control it, may feel like your personal Everest. Speaking from experience, claiming agency over the ability to control your attention in these circumstances is indeed a crucible. We will discuss the impacts of trauma in an upcoming chapter.

For now, here are three simple exercises to help you practice deliberately directing your attention. They can be used anywhere, anytime, so please employ them liberally.

Exercise 1: Find Your Safe Haven

1. Take a few relaxing deep breaths, focusing on your exhale.
2. With eyes closed, bring to mind either the memory of a safe place or an imaginary safe place where you felt, or can imagine yourself feeling, a deep sense of comfort, warmth, acceptance, ease, safety, freedom, peace, love, and joy. You may imagine yourself there alone or with others whom you feel safe to be your authentic self with.
3. Keep your attention there as long as you are able to. When it strays, return it back to this safe haven. Practice this for a few minutes at least two times each day, more if you can.

This exercise is basically the equivalent of teaching your attention the command "stay."

To give you an example, my imaginary safe haven is a long sandy beach on a beautiful sunny day. The sand is pristine white, as soft and fine as powder. Small waves roll gently up onto the beach. I imagine myself as a small child of about four years old, barefoot and scraggly-haired, running around playing joyfully in the sand and water with the four-year-old versions of my loved ones. Imagining us all that way, playful, innocent, and free, never fails to warm my heart, relax me, and put a big smile on my face.

Going to our safe haven is really a two-for-one deal. Not only will you be training your attention, but you'll also be getting the added benefits of reducing stress and flooding your body with natural feel-good chemicals.

Exercise 2: Internal and External Focus

1. Take a few relaxing deep breaths, focusing on your exhale.
2. Close your eyes or relax your gaze.
3. Spend about thirty seconds focusing your attention internally on a sensation in an area of your body or on the surface of your body, such as the sensation of your abdomen expanding with each breath, your tongue touching the roof of your mouth, the warmth of the sun on your face, or the breeze lightly tickling your bare arms.
4. Now, for another thirty seconds, shift to focusing your attention on something external, such as a noise in the environment, a scent in the air, or the hum of the neighbor's lawn mower.
5. Repeat steps three and four for three to five cycles one or more times per day. You can use a timer for this exercise if you find it helpful.

As an example, I might take a few breaths to help relax myself, close my eyes, then focus intently on feeling my heart beating. Rhythmic, warm, proudly orchestrating the show. I'd really get into the subtleties of the sensation. After about thirty seconds, I could shift my focus to the smell of pizza cooking in my oven (hell yeah!). Again, I'd be focusing on noticing the subtleties of the sensory information I was receiving, but this time from outside of my body. Continuing with these two sensations, one internal, one external, I would repeat this cycle three to five times. When I came back for another round later in the day, I would choose different sensations to focus on, both internally and externally.

This exercise is the next level of practice, in which you learn to shift your attention back and forth from internal to external focus at will. According to Dr. Michael McGee, author of the best-selling book *The Joy of Recovery: A Path to Freedom from Addiction*, interoception, or the ability to be aware of internal sensations in the body, is "the critical first step for accessing emotions, which live in the body."

This exercise is also a two-for-one deal, then! We cannot connect with our authentic selves if we cannot connect with our bodies and the emotions stored in them. So, not only are we training our attention with this exercise, but we're also laying the foundation for practicing interoception more easily as we progress into befriending our bodies and emotions in future chapters.

Exercise 3: Find Five Things

1. Think of something you would like more of in your experience, something you'd like to magnify by focusing your attention on it.
2. Right now, or throughout the day, write down five things you notice that are "evidence" of its general existence.

3. Do this with as many items as you want, and as many times throughout the day as you want, but be sure to do it with at least one item at least once per day.

For example, if you wanted vibrant health, you would make it your mission to find five things that provide proof that vibrant health exists. If you cannot find things that feel good to notice about your specific health, you can look for signs of vibrant health in the world around you.

A specific list might look like:

- My heart is beating solidly.
- My breathing is happening without me having to think about it.
- I slept well.
- I have a good amount of energy today.
- My immune system is working behind the scenes fighting off all sorts of things I don't even know about.

A more general list might look like:

- Babies keep being born.
- My neighbor was really going after it working in her garden today.
- That dancer is strong and fit.
- Those children on the playground have boundless energy.
- Many people were shopping at the organic fruit stand I just passed.

The idea, again, is that what we want to experience more of is already all around us; we just need to train our brains to look for evidence to support it, rather than evidence that contradicts it. It's easy to find whichever you choose to look for; we've just been deeply conditioned to look for proof of struggle and scarcity. Engaging in this exercise regularly over time will help you teach your brain to instead automatically find proof of possibility and abundance.

The Ultimate Leverage

Yes, training your attention with exercises like this is a bit of work at first, but as your brain creates the new neural pathways to support this new skill, wielding your attention deliberately will become more and more like second nature. You will teach your brain what is important for it to focus on and, as brains do, your brain will naturally make you more aware of that which you have bookmarked as "Important!" Again, if you're a trauma survivor, you will likely have quite a bit of deeper emotional work to do as you learn to gain control of your attention. This work cannot be bypassed, nor would you want to. As Carl Jung, Swiss psychiatrist and founder of analytical psychology, famously wrote, "Until you make the unconscious conscious, it will direct your life, and you will call it fate." Thus, I hope the idea of liberating yourself from being at the mercy of the conditioned responses of unaddressed trauma can serve as even more motivation for you to practice this work consistently.

As you become adept, you'll gain the ability to shift your attention quickly away from what you don't want to magnify in your experience and toward what you do want to magnify in your experience. In a world where you can train your brain to magnify literally anything you want it to, why not train it to spend only as much time on the shit sandwiches in life as is absolutely needed to process them, and to then turn its attention to things that don't make you miserable?

As a simple experiment, you could train your brain to pay attention to the sounds of birds chirping. Just by mentally bookmarking the sounds of birds as important, you will be unable to help but notice significantly more birdsong in your day-to-day experience. It was there all along, but now you've learned to "collapse the wave function" with your focused attention and magnify birdsong in your experience. Just in writing this, I have myself become aware of the distinctive song of a particularly vocal bird that's perched happily in a tree outside my office window. The bird has most likely been there all morning, but I was previously unconscious of it because I had been choosing to place my attention on other things.

This bookmarking for magnification, so to speak, can (and should) be done with anything that is important to you. Harnessing the power of your attention is an absolute *force multiplier* when it comes to inviting anything you want more of into your experience, including self-love, self-compassion, and self-acceptance. Train your brain to focus on what you want more of. If you want a good relationship with yourself, train your brain to focus on what you want more of in that relationship. This is our superpower as humans. You will have to train it consistently, but just like you wouldn't want to let your new puppy keep peeing all over the floor, you don't want to let yourself go through life with sloppy focus.

Consistency Pays Off

Thankfully, when my new desire hatched at that meeting, I was able to draw on prior learning and wield my own attention wisely. I'd held myself back too many times in the past and frankly, I was tired of how *bad* it felt. Instead, I decided to take the path of believing that anything is possible, that stranger things have happened, and that things would work out in my favor. I forced my fear-conditioned mind to get in the back seat and pipe down. I imagined myself having the job, let myself *feel* what it would be like having it, and allowed myself to contentedly live there in my imagination without telling stories about why it might not happen for me. I allowed myself to know that all the necessary elements were coalescing behind the scenes. I didn't try to figure out the "how" or "when." I just chilled out, enjoyed the simple relief of letting myself focus on possibility instead of fear, and let go of attachment to any certain outcome. As opportunities that felt good and seemed as though they could help move me in the direction of my desire arose, I took action. Sometimes this called for a significant investment of my time and energy. I invested it happily.

Eighteen months later, I was signing the employment offer for the *newly created* position of statewide training coordinator for that team. They actually *did* create a brand-new position! Can you believe it? I had to go through a rigorous interview process, but I got the job. It was so face-meltingly awesome to witness how becoming the boss of my attention led to the actualization of my big, seemingly impossible desire. The uplevel in empowerment I felt as a result of seeing this eighteen-month creative process bear fruit was transformative for me. I've been in the position for almost three years, at the time of this writing, and the work has been an even more fulfilling experience than I ever imagined it would be.

This is just one small example of the incredible power of harnessing your attention and using it deliberately. Even with consistency, your desired results probably won't happen overnight, and bringing them to fruition will require action on your part, but I promise you, it will be *one million percent* worth it.

3
Meditate

The least comfortable moments in our lives are often our most powerful wake-up calls.

Let me tell you a story about one.

I stepped out of the shower and leaned up against the wall in exhaustion. My legs didn't want to hold me up, so I just sort of crumpled into a heap on the bath mat. Resting my head back on the wall behind me, I let out what felt like the deepest sigh in history.

I'd been awake all night, lying in bed, staring wide-eyed at the ceiling, stewing in white-hot rage after an argument *royale* with my husband. It had started with him pushing buttons. Hard. It ended with me straddling his chest in bed at three in the morning, screaming obscenities while windmilling my arms at him.

Not my best moment.

He's about twice my size, so he had only to hold up a forearm to deflect my hysterical swatting. He did so while laughing in my face with contemptuous amusement. As you can imagine, this did not make me less angry. We weren't typically fighters, as a couple, but *that* fight, now branded "the fight-heard-round-the-world," could easily have ended our marriage.

In the light of day, there on my bathroom floor the next morning, I felt completely lost. I knew that this was *not* the kind of relationship dynamic I wanted to be in. This wasn't the kind of *life* I wanted to live. I was not being the *person* I wanted to be. The moment had a very ... rock-bottomy feel to it. I knew things needed to change, but I had no idea where to start.

I closed my eyes, listening to the hum of the ceiling fan, and let myself float off mentally. I may have briefly dozed off; I don't know. What I do know is that I managed to find an unlikely sliver of relief there that morning on my bathroom floor. The next morning when I got out of the shower, I decided to sit down on the bath mat again. Okay, it's a weird place to chill, I know, but I was still an emotional dumpster fire, and I knew no one would bother me there. Maybe it would work again? I just needed some relief. *Any* relief. The bath mat did not disappoint. So, the next day, I did it again. A little more relief. And the next day I did it again.

I wasn't hiding out on my bathroom floor morning after morning with the intent of starting a daily meditation practice. I was just so desperate to feel better that I didn't know what else to do. I was clinging to anything that helped even a little. This is how my daily meditation habit kind of snuck up on me. As the days went on, I started to feel noticeably better, so I just kept repeating the behavior. I felt lighter, more free, more peaceful. I had a new sense of clarity and well-being. I also noticed that the feeling lasted beyond the mat, allowing me to go out into my day in a much better headspace. I also noticed that my intuition was becoming sharper, and little things started lining up for me with a kind of synchronicity I couldn't explain. Most surprisingly, I started to feel a less pronounced but more prolonged version of the euphoric sense of connection I described in Chapter One. I can only describe the sensation as *wholeness.* Utter wholeness. Meditation seemed to be giving me a feeling of being somehow ... *tapped in*. I was intrigued.

When I was deep in meditation, my perception of time, my body, and my individual identity often faded away. I could viscerally *feel* my personal energy field's resonance and oneness with the primordial energy field. And in case you were about to ask, no, I was not on drugs.

Game Changer

While it probably doesn't seem like sitting down and chilling out would be such a big deal, gettin' cozy with the intelligent force that is continually creating everything in existence turns out to be the ultimate game-changer.

"If meditation is so powerful and easy, why isn't everyone doing it?" you might be wondering. Good question! We can (and do) make all kinds of excuses for not taking the time to connect with the source of our authentic selves, the most popular excuse being "I don't have time." Let's get real, folks. I cannot think of one single person I know, including myself, who couldn't afford to subvert just a *fraction* of the time they spend with their face glued to their smartphone or laptop and use it instead to, oh I don't know, tap into the power source that gives them *life*, in addition to creating the universe and everything in it.

Another hang-up many people have around starting a daily meditation practice is that they give themselves analysis paralysis. "Which style of meditation should I choose?" "Guided or not guided?" "How long do I need to meditate for?" Unless you're already happily practicing a distinct style of meditation that works for you, don't let any of those details distract you from the real goal, which is simply to sit down and slow down long enough to tap into the source of your power. There is no "right" or "wrong" way to meditate. Some people enjoy guided meditations to start, some people like to focus on their breath, some people love a good chant ... It's perfectly all right to experiment in order to find your groove. We each get to do what feels right for us. That may also change over time. No problem. You really can't get it wrong, *unless you don't do it.*

The best first step is to just sit down, silence thyself, silence thy cell phone, and get started gathering some experiential data of your own. Here are the absolute basics:

1. Find a quiet place free from distractions. White noise can be helpful for drowning out audible distractions.
2. Set a timer, if desired. Start with five minutes if you're new to meditation and work your way up to twenty or more minutes per day over the course of a few weeks.
3. Sit or lie down in a comfortable position and close your eyes. Make sure you have whatever you need to keep your body temperature in a comfortable range.
4. Take a few deep, slow breaths, allow your muscles to relax, then continue to focus your attention on your breathing. Let it flow in and out naturally.
5. Finally, don't bother trying to wrestle your mind into silence. It will never shut all the way off unless you're unconscious, or dead (and maybe not even then, for all we know). Silencing your thoughts completely is not the point. *Witnessing* your conditioned mind doing its gymnastics without judgment is the point. Each time you notice yourself following some random thought tangent, you can just say to yourself silently, lovingly, and non-judgmentally, "thinking," and then return your attention to your breath.

There's really no need to make it more complicated than that if you're just getting started. Your meditation session is your one precious and rare opportunity each day to *rest*, save when you're sleeping. It's a time when you can get a brief and glorious reprieve from the inner critic, and when you are not obligated to give any craps about what's going on outside of you. Instead of frantically trying to solve things, fix things, and control things, you get to take a *break* that's just for you and become the gentle observer of your existence, experiencing the sweet relief of letting it all go and remembering that *you are not your thoughts*. You are the witnesser. You are learning to be the director.

Meditation may seem too simple a path to freedom from the mental chaos most of us live in most of the time, and from the drama we create around it, but it *works*. As sixteenth-century physicist and scholar Blaise Pascal so aptly put it, "All of man's troubles stem from his inability to sit quietly in a room alone." I couldn't agree more. That is what this book is about, after all. Learning to be with our authentic selves in peaceful, compassionate non-judgment.

With regular daily practice, you will gradually start to feel a deep sense of wholeness, freedom, and relief. Physically, you may feel floaty or warm or tingly. You may experience spontaneous chills or tears of relief or gratitude. A sense of being unconditionally loved and supported may begin to permeate your life. Or you might feel nothing out of the ordinary for a long time, besides incredibly relaxed. Try to be patient and let go of expectations. There is nothing to prove. Please, please, *please* don't let this turn into another thing you berate yourself for because you don't think you're doing it "right." If you're *doing it*, then you're doing it well enough.

People's experiences differ, but one thing people who practice meditation regularly *do* share is that once they realize just how good they can feel, nothing else will do. There is no going back. They don't *want* to go back, nor do they need to summon motivation to sit in daily meditation. They *crave* it, because it is the best part of their day, every day.

No Looking Back

Many years into a daily meditation practice, *nothing* in my life is the same. My physical and emotional health, my relationships, my career, my finances—all have been radically transformed for the better. I feel truly present in my life, which is the biggest gift of all. If I had known what a drastic difference meditation would make in my life, I would have started *decades* ago!

If you're ready to delve into meditation or supplement your existing practice, and would like to explore a curated list of guided meditations to help you get started, please go to www.whyconnectingworks.com/bookbonuses and navigate to the Authentic Connection Book Bonuses section. There you will find some of my personal favorite tried-and-true guided meditations.

As you develop your meditation practice, you too will become progressively more aware of positive transformations happening in your life, above and beyond simply *allowing*

yourself to feel good, which (if we're being honest) may be a pretty big change itself. You'll notice that your thoughts, attitudes, words, and behaviors will begin to gradually and naturally shift to align with feeling good more of the time, even when you're not "on the mat." Eventually, you will no longer have to coerce yourself into doing your daily meditation. You will jump at the opportunity. You will feel like you have been given the keys to the kingdom. However, consistently practicing mediation will simply show you that you have held the keys inside you all along.

4
Reflect

"I can shake off everything as I write;
my sorrows disappear, my courage is reborn."
—Anne Frank

Reflective writing, AKA "journaling," once saved me from having a meltdown of historic proportions.

One day, out of the blue, in March of his senior year in high school, my 18-year-old son announced that he was moving out of our family home and into a condo with one of his friends. Like, *next week*.

I had been operating under the assumption that he would be living at home for at least a few more months, until the end of the school year, so naturally I was a bit shocked. I held myself together outwardly and was somehow able to discuss his decision with him in a calm, rational conversation. I could tell he'd given his decision a lot of thought. Besides, the condo was really nice, and the rent was a screaming deal. It was clear that he was itching to "get on with his life," and I certainly recalled myself feeling more than ready to spread my wings at that age.

I gave him my blessing.

Inside, however, I was *unraveling*.

Sheer. Panic.

Had I done enough as a parent? Would he ever call me? Would I ever see him again? Would he be able to fend for himself in the world? What if he got lonely? Would he eat a *single* vegetable?!

At this point, I should probably confess that the condo he was planning to move into was seven minutes away.

I know, I know, but if you haven't been the parent of a child leaving home for the first time, you can just *shoosh* with your judgment, okay? If you *have* been a parent in this position, you know intimately that when your child leaves home it is anything but a "rational" emotional experience and that my hysterics were completely normal.

Clinging to the cliff edge of sanity, I turned to a practice I'd always counted on to soothe me: writing. I got out my journal and wrote and wrote and wrote and wrote.

Why Writing?

Reflective writing is one of the most powerful tools we can use, not only for self-soothing but also for cultivating self-awareness, connecting with our authentic selves, and focusing our attention. It allows us to corral and sort our wild, chaotic thoughts so we can get back in the saddle, holding the reins. Reflective writing allows us to collect and record "experiential data" that can prove to be very illuminating. When we deliberately choose our thoughts and train our attention, writing about it reinforces the newly developing pathways in our brains, thereby strengthening them over time. It's just another powerful mechanism for training your brain to do what you want it to do.

Here are a few reflective writing exercises that I have found to be highly effective over the years. I hope they will help you get started:

Exercise 1: Today I Noticed ...

Get cozy with your journal or laptop and write down some things that you noticed about your thinking, your emotions, and your behaviors during the day. Alternatively, you could even use the notes app on your phone to write things down throughout the day as you're noticing them. It can be useful to give yourself a small, manageable goal for this exercise, such as reflecting on three things each day that you noticed about your internal processing and how it correlated to your behavior or vice versa.

Exercise 2: Worst Case/Best Case

This is a great reflection exercise that I learned from life coach and author Andrew Leedham's fantastic book, *Unstoppable Self Confidence*. I find it very useful when I am feeling plagued by indecision about how to proceed on something, or if I find myself catastrophizing or stuck in rumination about something. It's a way to step back and take a rational look at a situation, so your brain can stop freaking out and trying to sabotage you. First, write about what the worst-case scenario would look like, were it to happen. Next, write about what the best-case scenario would look like for this situation. Finally, genuinely reflect on these two questions: What benefit(s) do I derive from focusing on the worst-case scenario? What benefit(s) do I derive from focusing on the best-case scenario? *Realistically*, where do I think things are likely to land on that spectrum regarding this situation?

Exercise 3: What's Working?

This exercise never fails to turn my focus back toward all the things that are working out in my life if I realize I'm veering toward Self-Pity City, or even if I just want to summon some good feelings of appreciation and gratitude to enhance an already decent mood. It's super simple. Just start listing things that are working out well for you. You can stay present tense or include things from the past that worked well. You can go very general such as "I woke up this morning" (bonus!), or you can get really granular such as "the jeans I have on today really make my booty pop," or anywhere in between. This exercise can be applied broadly, but it can also be applied to something particular you would like to examine more closely. Looking at what is working can help bring some relief to situations that you feel are currently in the gutter, or it can just help you lock in your existing glee in areas where you're already flourishing. If you're feeling really bold, I would challenge you to take it a step further and reflect on this question: "What *problems* in my life are actually working in some ways for me? In what (even small) ways are they benefiting me?"

Exercise 4: If You Already Knew ...

In one of his courses, renowned author and speaker Dr. Joe Dispenza asked the following questions that became the basis for this reflective writing exercise for me. He asked, "What would change if you already knew your prayers had been answered? Who would you be? How would you live?" This question was so intriguing to me that when I heard it, I dropped everything and started writing about it on the spot. I apply the word "prayer" loosely, preferring to not take the question literally, but more for its spirit, which I feel to be "What would change if you knew that everything you want and need was completely taken care of and you didn't have to worry about anything? Who would you be? How would you live?" Whatever phrasing works best for you is fine. What's most important is that you contemplate this thoroughly, be honest with yourself, and write the responses that flow out of you naturally.

Exercise 5: Love Letter to Little You

There's been a real swell in popularity of what I would call the "re-parenting movement" over the last couple of decades. Re-parenting is about connecting with your inner child and re-parenting yourself from your adult perspective, being the safe and loving caregiver to your inner child who may have been absent, abusive, checked out, or neglectful to you when you were a child, when you had no way of blunting or understanding the impacts of the harmful situation on yourself.

We're not going to delve into exploring our attachment wounds, processing trauma, or re-parenting work in this book. Not only is it beyond the scope of this book, but I also believe that type of work should initially be explored with the guidance of a trained and licensed mental health professional, which I am not. I bring it up only as context, but do encourage you to explore these interrelated topics further if they intrigue you.

For the purpose of this writing exercise, I'm just going to ask you to spend a little time sending loving remarks and stories about what it's like to be an adult to your inner child via writing them a letter. To begin, take a few moments to close your eyes, breathe deeply, and imagine yourself as a small, sweet, innocent child, untouched by pain, shame, fear, guilt, emotional wounds, and heartache. See yourself in a peaceful, safe place where you feel happy and free. Once you've connected deeply with this young version of yourself, open your eyes and write Little You a letter. You may just say hello and ask Little You if they would tell you about themselves. Psychologists often recommend writing *to* your inner child with your dominant hand and writing the responses you receive *from* your inner child with your nondominant hand in an attempt to forcibly slow the adult brain down a bit and engage in bilateral stimulation, which, it is theorized, may make you more open to accessing deeply stored emotions. Alternatively, you may share stories about your life now as an adult with this adorable, untainted little soul. If unmanageable feelings arise in you for any reason while doing this writing exercise, please pause the exercise and seek the care of a mental health professional or call the mental health crisis line by dialing 9-8-8.

If you would like to see examples of any of these writing exercises to get your brain juices flowing and explore additional valuable reflective writing exercises, please go to the bonus book resources at www.whyconnectionworks.com/bookbonuses and navigate to the Authentic Connection Book Bonuses section.

A New Chapter

All the writing I did in the week before my son moved out helped me process the pain of coming to the "end of his childhood." Instead of avoiding my emotions by drinking myself into oblivion or bypassing them with fake positivity, reflective writing allowed me to explore them self-compassionately. Only after doing this emotional processing was I able to turn my attention to the possibilities of this new, exciting chapter for both of us. It helped me calibrate to the feeling of both of us growing and thriving. I was able to shift into seeing more expanded and hopeful horizons for both of us instead of fixating solely on the void he would leave behind. I'm not going to lie and say that it 100 percent kept me from pacing and crying, but it sure helped a lot.

I actually ended up compiling some of my journal excerpts from that week into a small handwritten "book" for him, a little parting gift from mother to son. I filled it with inspiring quotes and nuggets of wisdom I'd picked up along my forty-some years on the trail. He seemed to appreciate it. If nothing else, it felt good to give him a physical token of my love and care that he could take with him as he embarked on his own life adventure.

What Will You Try?

If you can only carve out a little time to write each day, perhaps the exercises I shared would be fun to put on a rotation. Or maybe there's one in particular that speaks to you? Maybe you'll choose to freewrite. It's *all* good. Putting pen to paper and seeing what comes out is the most important part.

Wait ... but what if someone *sees* it?! (Gasp!)

Sometimes people feel like they need to censor their writing, in case someone else should ever read it, then judge and ridicule them or share their private ponderings. Whatever you do, do *not* censor yourself when writing. It defeats the entire purpose of reflective writing, which is to commune with your authentic (uncensored) self. Consider that this may be the *only* space in your life in which you get to be completely yourself. It may be the only space in which you feel free to admit what your heart truly wants. If the thought of someone reading what you've written worries you, buy a journal with a lock, or do whatever you must to destroy the damning evidence of your hideous desire for self-reflection once you're done writing. In the *act* of reflective writing, you've already received its major benefits. Keeping your writing in perpetuity is not a requirement, unless it pleases you to do so. I personally refuse to censor myself when I engage in reflective writing and have stacks and stacks of old journals lying around my bedroom and home office. If someone has the audacity to violate my privacy by cracking one open, they get what they get. Sorry, not sorry.

I encourage you to embrace this brazen attitude if it suits you. It's kind of liberating. Either way, I hope you start your reflective writing practice today, in whatever way you see fit, so you can start connecting deeply with your authentic self and experience all the benefits it will bring to your life.

5
Befriend Your Body

I very much remember relating to something the gifted author Jen Sincero once wrote, describing how we tend to ignore and neglect our bodies in our endless search for more and more, paying them little respect and basically dragging them around behind us like "old tattered wind socks."

If we're discussing how I treated my body the first forty-ish years of its life, dragging it around like "an old tattered wind sock" is probably a *generous* metaphor. I was generally running around so frantic and stressed out that I was barely conscious of *having* a body.

Genetically, I am lucky in that I inherited a naturally strong and healthy constitution. As such, I just sort of expected my body to put up with whatever I ordered it to do and never complain. In fact, I was so used to taking my health and mobility for granted in my youth that I think I developed a fairly delusional sense of indestructibility and imperviousness to physical deterioration. I pushed and pushed myself, harder and harder, year after year, decade after decade, with very little regard to the potential long-term health consequences of doing so.

It wasn't until a global pandemic slowed down our rat-race paced, more-more-more lifestyle long enough for me to really listen to my body that I realized I was utterly physically exhausted and in complete adrenal burnout. I had to admit to myself that I *for real* had a toxic relationship with alcohol and that I was slowly losing my battle to control it. I also had to admit to myself that the escalating sciatic nerve issue I'd been ignoring was going to continue derailing my fitness efforts if I didn't address it. That irritated me because, to be honest, I had been kind of counting on my fitness efforts to magically cancel out the damage of decades of abusing my body.

I didn't want to see any of these realities. In fact, I'd been doing a damn fine job of running away from them up until that point. As previously mentioned, wake-up calls are not typically that comfortable. But, once I finally reached acceptance, I realized I had backed myself into a corner. It was either give up the unmitigated stress and the alcohol or give up everything else I wanted in my life, like my liver. I had to make a choice. Unless I was okay with rusting away like the Tin Man and falling apart a piece at time, I was going to have to start taking real responsibility for my health.

Respect Your Home

How we feel emotionally is as much a product of our physical health as it is our mental health. We feel our best when our mental and physical processes are working together harmoniously. Our physical bodies do miraculous things. They are our homes on this planet. Yet, we very rarely give them all the things they need to function most effectively. In fact, we often actively abuse them.

Often, we treat them like dumpsters, pouring and stuffing and puffing into them whatever toxic crap we want to. We abuse our bodies by neglecting them and ignoring the signals they try to give us to tell us what they need. We abuse our bodies by judging, critiquing, comparing, and hating them. We abuse our bodies by chronically forcing them to function at high stress levels. We do all this, then we act surprised, and even victimized, when they become diseased and start to break down.

If you want to develop a connection with your authentic self, meeting your body's basic physical health needs and treating it with respect is paramount. Loving and appreciating it is even better! We have a tendency to think of our minds as separate from our bodies, but really, our bodies and minds are in this thing together.

Here are some practices you can try to give your body respect and appreciation and help it to function optimally, which will have a natural and sustainable positive impact on how you feel emotionally.

Hydrate well

Drink plenty of the cleanest water you have access to each day, first thing in the morning and between meals. Having a water habit can be helpful. For example, I fill up two water bottles each morning that together hold 80 ounces of water and make it my goal to finish drinking them both each day.

Sleep more

Try to log at *least* seven hours per night whenever possible. As a former insomniac, I can attest that, however unlikely this may seem, it is possible if you are willing to provide yourself with the proper conditions and persevere. If you'd like to download my free Sleep Rescue Guide and learn how to become an excellent sleeper, visit www.whyconnectionworks.com/bookbonuses and navigate to the Authentic Connection Book Bonuses section.

Allow yourself to rest

Napping is not a sin. It helps us function better. Our bodies need periodic rest because we are not robots. That said, it took me a long time and more therapy than I care to admit to train my brain into being able to take even a short nap during the day without having extreme anxiety. I understand it may not feel that natural, or maybe even safe, to allow ourselves rest in this fast-paced modern world. Additionally, most of us don't often have the luxury of a *long* rest break during the day, but even a quick 10–20 minute meditation or power nap is enough time for the brain and body to feel a little more refreshed. If you do have the time to take a longer break and a nap feels good, definitely go for it! Rest can only do good things for your brain and body.

Move your body

You've probably heard it said that "Sitting is the new smoking." That's because the functioning of every system in your body benefits from regular movement during waking hours. Being sedentary as a lifestyle wreaks havoc on our physical and mental health. You don't have to go bananas at the gym if that's not your thing. This can be functional movement, like taking the stairs, biking to the office, playing with your kids or pets, working in your garden, or cleaning house. It's just important that you spend plenty of time moving, period. I have to be really diligent about this personally, because I have a "desk job." I try to stand at my desk as much as possible. I wiggle. I fidget. I try to take small movement breaks between meetings, get outside for a walk or jog in the morning or on my lunch break, and forcefully try to keep myself from flopping on the couch right after work by making dinner, doing yard work, taking a walk, or finding other active things to do.

Stop treating your body like a dumpster

Processed foods are terrible for the brain and body. I'm not saying I never eat them or that you should never eat them, because that's probably not very realistic. What I am saying is, with the standard addition of excessive sugar, sodium, unhealthy oils, artificial colors, flavors, and sweeteners, all of which have been scientifically proven to cause health problems, processed foods are something we should try to minimize if we want our bodies to function well and if we want to feel well.

Alcohol and other drugs are also terrible for the brain and body, even when consumed in "moderate" amounts. Again, I'm not throwing stones here—I've consumed plenty of alcohol and other drugs in my life—I'm just stating facts. They are toxic for our brains and bodies and should be minimized or eliminated if we want our bodies to function well and if we want to feel well long term. If you're interested in learning more about the body of research about alcohol's effects on our brains and bodies, I encourage you to listen to the *Huberman Lab Podcast* episode entitled "What Alcohol Does to Your Body, Brain, and Health." Warning: you can't unhear what you hear, so if you're trying to stay in denial about alcohol's terrifying effects on health, you'll definitely not want to listen to it. Personally, I will be forever grateful that Dr. Huberman was bold enough to have some real talk with his audience about the research on how alcohol affects the brain. Hearing it was pivotal in helping cement my resolve to create a lifestyle that supports my passion for lifelong learning.

Develop body awareness

Instead of running completely on autopilot, try taking a few moments here and there throughout your day to check in with your body. Close your eyes, take a deep breath, and give it a little head-to-toe scan. What is it doing? What is it feeling? Are there corresponding emotions that you can identify? Where do you feel them in your body? What needs your attention?

Stop criticizing your body

Whether out loud or internally, criticizing your body is harmful. In fact, it's self-abuse. Your body's just trying to help you live, which is kind of awesome of it. Instead of hating on the parts of your body you don't like, try shifting your attention to picking out things you *do* like or appreciate about your body, in function or appearance. Do you have nice eyes? A warm smile? Cute freckles? Do you appreciate how you are able to haul your groceries inside? How good it feels to sing or dance? Our bodies are all kinds of miraculous if we really take a moment to think about them.

Stop judging your body against unattainable and arbitrary "beauty" standards

This is the number one way to support the previous recommendation of not criticizing your body. There is no such thing as a "perfect" body, only the ever-shifting mirage of the "perfect" body projected by the multibillion-dollar cosmetic and diet industries to keep us consuming their products in a futile effort to get our bodies closer to looking like the current image of the "perfect" body. I'm not saying you should never alter your body. Your body is *yours* to exist in, in any way that you choose to. You do you. I'm just suggesting that the way you choose to live in your body be based on wanting to celebrate your joy for existing in your body, not on judging it against the media's arbitrary and unattainable beauty standards.

Downshift

When we're chronically overstressed, everything in our brains and bodies gets thrown out of whack, which leads to adverse mental and physical health outcomes. Unfortunately, our culture has become a breeding ground of chronic stress. We're constantly running around, overscheduling, overworking, and demanding ever more of ourselves. And for what? So we can feel anxious all the time and secretly want to escape our daily lives? This is no way to live. I encourage you to take your power back and prioritize reducing chronic stress in your life. Don't live at work, don't commit to a bunch of extra committees and events, don't put your kids in every single sport and activity, say no to things you don't want to do, stay at a hotel when visiting family if you tend to feel best with some privacy and downtime, and so on. Little by little, the out-of-control momentum of your life will decrease to a more reasonable pace, and you'll be so much healthier and happier for it.

Practice nervous system self-regulation

When we are faced with acute, unmanageable stress, acute trauma, the reactivation of past trauma, or the chronic activation of complex trauma, our nervous systems switch into survival mode functioning. This aspect of our nervous system is also known as the sympathetic nervous system. The sympathetic nervous system's job is to prepare our bodies for strenuous action.

When activated, it quickly floods our body with the surge of adrenaline it needs to fight or flee from a perceived threat. Many other things simultaneously occur, including an increase in heart rate, blood pressure, perspiration, and pupil dilation. We may begin feeling intensely agitated or combative. When this happens, other functions of the nervous system, such as digestion and higher-order brain functions, are deactivated, to a degree.

Meaning, if you're staring down a grizzly bear in the woods, your nervous system will immediately divert its resources *away* from nervous system activities that could slow you down, like digesting, analyzing, and problem-solving, and *toward* nervous system activities that will support fighting or fleeing, should it become necessary. This is often referred to as hyper-arousal.

If fighting or fleeing from the perceived threat is not an option, we may then shift into what is referred to as hypo-arousal. In *hypo*-arousal, we will either freeze ("play dead" or shut down) or fawn (behave in ways that will hopefully appease the threatening party). You will sometimes hear this sympathetic nervous system pattern referred to as "fight, flight, freeze, fawn" or "fight, flight, freeze, appease." Being in either a state of hyper- or hypo-arousal is often referred to as being "dysregulated."

The reason I bring all this up is that, even though we're not facing a lot of grizzly bears these days, many of us are so used to operating at chronically high stress levels we don't even realize we are in a near constant state of low-grade sympathetic nervous system activation, which leads to adverse physical and mental health effects over time. Specifically, chronic anxiety, depression, and extreme burnout anhedonia, which is a lack of ability to feel pleasure from life's experiences.

Being activated by an *acutely* stressful event or trauma trigger is also very uncomfortable. In either case, a major component of befriending your body is learning how to soothe yourself when you notice that you are becoming activated. Be on the lookout for signs of both hyper- and hypo-arousal. Some common hyper-arousal signs to look out for are rising anxiety levels, pounding heart, hyper-vigilance, heightened sensitivity to noise and light, irritability, anger, combativeness, heavy breathing, palms sweating, and restlessness. Probably the most common *hypo*-arousal signs to look out for are spacing out, emotional numbness, lethargy, and depression.

You can't really think your way out of a stress response, since it short-circuits higher order thinking functions of the brain, but there are many effective "bottom up" body-focused techniques that you can employ to help you regulate your nervous system and bring your frontal lobe back online when you become aware that you are feeling dysregulated. Here is a short and by no means exhaustive list of techniques. What you choose will be individual, based on what you find effective and enjoy doing:

- Bilateral stimulation
- Deep breathing
- Smelling relaxing essential oils
- Humming, singing, or chanting
- Progressive muscle relaxation

- Pacing, rocking, or swaying
- Meditation
- Yin yoga
- Enjoyable exercise
- Listening to soothing music
- Engaging in arts or crafts
- Dancing
- Getting a massage
- Hanging out with a loved one
- Cuddling
- Relaxing in nature
- Petting your dog or cat

What sounds most relaxing to you? How might you be able to incorporate one or more of these self-regulation techniques into situations in which you know you tend to feel mildly or even highly dysregulated?

Homecoming

When I took a good look at how I was really treating my body, it became evident that I had been very detached from it for a very long time. While being detached from my body had been an adaptive strategy in the past, I knew it had become maladaptive in recent years and that it was time for me to come home to my body, start treating it like the miracle that it is, and fully integrate with it. There were a number of areas that I knew I could make changes in that would greatly benefit my physical, mental, and emotional health.

First and most importantly, I made the commitment to work on my relationships with alcohol and its faithful sidekick, nicotine. I finally saw them for what they were, the most well-worn tools in my Numb and Avoid Toolkit. Pernicious, societally condoned methods of slow suicide. Recovering from any compulsive emotional numbing behavior is not typically a linear process. Periods of abstinence spackled with occasional flare ups of symptoms are certainly par for the recovery course for those with severe substance or alcohol use disorders. This was true for me too, but over the course of about two years, with the help of medication for addiction treatment, skilled behavioral health professionals, and some serious perseverance I was able to gain real traction in recovery.

I also realized that I had been at war with my body's natural rhythm of needing a rest during the late afternoon. In fact, for years I had been beating myself up each afternoon when my brain and body would get squirrely on me around 2 or 3 p.m. One day I had an epiphany: maybe I should listen to my body and try to just give it what it needed when it needed it, instead of trying to ignore it and push through the discomfort. I noticed that pushing through it only resulted in me producing lesser-quality work and defaulting to internally berating myself, letting the nasty internal voice tell me I was a lazy, unfocused piece of crap, even though during all other parts of the day I had no trouble working for hours on end with intense focus. My supervisor thought it made perfect sense when I told her that my brain functions best before 2 p.m., and therefore, I'd prefer to work through the morning until 2 p.m. and take a later than traditional lunch hour, since that was typically when my brain was demanding a rest anyway. I shifted into that schedule the following afternoon and have never looked back. Not only do I produce more high-quality work earlier in the day when my brain is fresh and focused, I also get to get up and move around, do some meditation, or go take a power nap in the afternoon when my brain needs a break. Then, I can return to my work focused and refreshed. Oh, and I no longer internally berate myself for being a lazy, unfocused piece of crap every day. Big win.

Outside of my workday, I also focused on making it a priority to meditate, exercise, get some fresh air and sunshine, drink lots of water, eat fruits and vegetables, have some fun, and get to bed at a reasonable time so I could get some good sleep.

Finally, I started the long process of ceasing a lifetime of poisoning myself with toxic thoughts about my body. At the time of this writing, I would say that I am still in the process of retraining my brain to default to loving and appreciating my body. I've been treating it well and taking good care of it and have made great progress in developing a healthy and mutually respectful relationship with it, *and* it's a deeply rooted pattern that I will probably have to work on for a long time.

Still, making these four shifts in how I treat my body has had an unspeakably positive impact on my physical, mental, and emotional health. Perhaps the biggest benefit is that I experience infinitely less anxiety on a daily basis. If you have ever lived with anxiety, you know just how priceless that is.

It is my most sincere hope that employing some or all of the practices in this chapter will help you nurture an authentic, respectful, and mutually beneficial relationship with your body so you can enjoy feeling good. For resources related to all the recommendations in this chapter, go to www.whyconnectionworks.com/bookbonuses and navigate to the Authentic Connection Book Bonuses section.

6
Be Your Own BFF

When I finally landed my dream job after more than twenty years of scrapping *hard* to get there, I was expecting to feel a sense of relief. Not only was I stoked about the job, but my new salary would also actually afford me the luxury of knowing that I could single-handedly provide for myself and my son, should the need ever arise, which had been one of my primary, lifelong objectives. Shouldn't there have been more of a sense of "I made it!"? *Some* sense that I could finally relax?

To my dismay, there was none. When I arrived at this milestone, I found that I was psychologically unable to allow myself even a moment to pause, rest, and enjoy the accomplishment. I was so yoked to the chronic sense of urgency my nervous system was used to that I could only focus on the *new* mountain of *new* projects that was towering before me. Instead of acknowledging all the grit, stamina, and tenacity I had summoned day after day, year after year, to earn this position, I berated myself for how long it took to get there. Worried I wouldn't be able to do the job well enough, I allowed myself to become totally consumed by the workload. In despair, I witnessed as I drove myself harder and harder, like a relentless jockey who would never be satisfied, no matter how far or how fast my horse ran, no matter how many finish lines I crossed.

Practice Self-Compassion

It never ceases to amaze me how terribly we tend to treat ourselves in comparison to how compassionately we tend to treat those around us. Most of us nearly continually criticize, shame, guilt, judge, blame, and otherwise trash-talk ourselves in our heads.

We look for approval outside of ourselves and let the presence or absence of it from others dictate how we feel about ourselves. We deprive ourselves of so many things because we feel unworthy and undeserving, and we refuse to forgive ourselves for past failures. We feel selfish and guilty for even *wanting* what we really want, never mind actually allowing ourselves to *have* it. After all, we wouldn't want to "get our hopes up." This ridiculous idea is how we've been programmed to think. We're implicitly given the message "Don't let yourself feel too good, in case later you might feel bad because you don't feel good anymore." Okay, *what*?! When good things do come into our lives, we often push them away or don't let ourselves fully enjoy them. We cautiously guard ourselves from feeling "too good" or getting "too excited" and instead superstitiously wait for "the other shoe to drop."

Public Service Announcement: *There is no other shoe.*

Imagine if you treated a friend this way! Telling them that you didn't think they were worthy or deserving of having nice things, resting, having fun, being loved, liking their body, or having what they want, no matter how hard they worked and sacrificed to earn it or how much they wanted it! They would ghost you instantly. I mean, who treats someone like that?!

I want you to imagine talking to a small, sweet, innocent four-year-old child the way you talk to yourself internally. When we were discussing the topic of abusive self-talk, a mentor once asked me, "Would you say those things to a small child?" I had an immediate visceral response of horror. "Of course not!" I said. I would *never* say those terrible things to a child because I know how much damage it would do to their psyche. I'm sure you wouldn't either.

Yet, we treat ourselves this way internally day in and day out and then wonder why we're not happier.

The hard truth is, there is nowhere to run from ourselves. Each of us lives and dies within our own minds, forever shackled to all the parts of ourselves that inhabit it. It's just you and *you* rattling around in there, forever. Why not befriend yourself?

In fact, let me rephrase that so it's not a question. I want you to commit right now to becoming your own best friend. I want you to practice witnessing your internal self-talk. When you catch yourself being mean to yourself, I want you to firmly tell your inner A-hole that it does *not* get to talk to your best friend that way!

This is *mission critical*. No one's going to come in there and love you *for* you. No one else can live inside your mind. *Loving you is an inside job.*

When you're struggling *and* when you're doing well, try to talk with yourself as if you are talking with your very best friend in the world or a sweet, innocent four-year-old child.

If they needed to rest, you wouldn't guilt them for it! You wouldn't passive-aggressively ask them, "Do you really think you should be spending time resting right now?" or "Wow, you're lazy." You'd say, "I'm so happy that you're taking good care of yourself!"

If they were absolutely crushing it in life, you wouldn't superstitiously warn them, "Well, don't get used to this. You'll probably screw this up. Remember, something always goes wrong for you. Everyone will find out you're an imposter soon enough." You'd say, "You deserve to have a kick-ass life because you're a kick-ass person!"

If they were going through a hard time, you wouldn't shame them by telling them, "You probably had this coming. If you weren't such a screw up, maybe your life wouldn't be so hard." No. You'd soothe them by saying things like "I'm so sorry you're going through this," "I'm here for you," "I believe in you," "How can I help?" and "You always have my support no matter what."

If they had the opportunity to have the shiny, wonderful new thing they'd been desperately wanting for a really long time, you wouldn't slap it out of their hands and say, "What makes you think you deserve that?" or "Everyone is going to think you're greedy for having that." You'd say, "I am *so incredibly happy* for you! This is awesome!" Then you'd jump up and down with them, like kids on a trampoline, squealing with glee.

But we say all of those awful things to ourselves, and more, don't we? Do you see how deeply harmful this is? Please, please, *please* promise me that you will start attempting to give yourself the same compassion, love, and grace you would extend to literally *anyone else* you loved. Clearly, self-compassion is a challenging practice to adopt. Fortunately, there are scientists making waves in this field, so we have more access than ever before to research, literature, resources, and tools to guide us on our journey to becoming self-compassionate. One of the most prominent researchers in the field, Dr. Kristin Neff, has a self-compassion research- and resource-rich website I strongly encourage you to explore at self-compassion.org.

See Through the Lies

"Worthy" and "unworthy" are constructs made by humans *for* humans. So are "deserving" and "undeserving." These ideas do not exist in relation to anything else in the natural world. Is one animal more worthy than another? Is one plant more deserving than another? Does a human infant come into this world inherently worthy or unworthy, deserving or undeserving? No, no, no, and no. Yet, we are all so steeped in these unhelpful, factless constructs that they are an unquestioned part of our collective subconscious programming and belief systems. They take root in our psyche as a result of needs going unmet in childhood and comparisons being made between ourselves and arbitrarily selected, and often unattainable, standards.

When one or more of our needs goes chronically unmet as an infant or young child, during early brain development when we do not yet have the intellectual capacity to reason *why* our needs are going unmet, we default to feeling that there must be something wrong with us, otherwise our caregiver would be meeting our needs. We then instinctively try harder to get the caregiver to meet our needs. This is an inherent survival mechanism. The problem is, it was never our fault that a caregiver didn't meet our needs, whether physical, emotional, or both, and no amount of striving to become more "worthy" of having our needs met on our part would have effected lasting change in the caregiver.

The human brain develops at an *incredibly* rapid pace in the first months and years of life. If an infant or toddler's needs go chronically unmet no matter what they do, their rapidly developing brain wires to believe that they must be unimportant or defective in some way. Even if a person's needs are met in infancy and toddlerhood, and their brain wires with a secure sense of their inherent worth, future neglect, abuse, and trauma can still disrupt the system and alter a person's perception of their worth.

Regardless of whether or not this was your experience in infancy, toddlerhood, or beyond, all humans in modernized societies are eventually thrust into a world of societally prescribed standards that define what is acceptable and what isn't, what is revered and what is reviled. It starts so young. Some of these ridiculous standards that we're automatically expected to uphold in order to be approved of and therefore to be considered "worthy" include, but are not limited to:

- Be a good girl.
- Be a good boy.
- Identify as either male or female.
- Be athletic.
- Be popular.
- Be thin.
- Be pretty.
- Be a people pleaser.
- Be a good student.
- Go to college.
- Accumulate material wealth to improve your status.
- If you're a woman, be sexy because that is where society and the media has told you your value lies, but don't be too sexy or overtly sexual, because then everyone will think you're a slut.
- If you're a man, don't have feelings.
- If you're a man, drink beer, play sports, watch sports, and don't wear pink.
- Be a monogamous heterosexual.
- Get married.
- Have children.
- Be religious.
- Do not differ from these standards either biologically or by choice, or you *will* be marginalized and discriminated against.

This is not an exhaustive list, as I'm sure you're aware, but we don't have all day. The point is, we are continually measured against standards such as these by society at large, and often by our families, and are overtly and covertly discriminated against if we don't "measure up" to one or more of them. This goes on until we ultimately internalize standards such as these and unconsciously measure *ourselves* against them. Then, if we feel we don't "measure up" to one or more of them, we decide that we are not "worthy" or "deserving," that there's something wrong with us, never stopping to consider that it might be the *standard* that is the issue (which it most definitely is).

The message I want you to take away from this rant is that there are no standards you have to measure up to in order to be "worthy" of anything. As speaker and author Esther Hicks has often said, "There is nothing to prove and no one to prove it to." You are as "worthy" or as "deserving" as anyone else is, simply as a function of being alive, of being an inseparable part of all that exists.

Stop Depriving Yourself

Now that we're done busting up the lies of worthiness and deservability, it's time to look at where in your life you may be unnecessarily depriving yourself based on those false constructs.

I really started to look at this myself when I had a few realizations about my own self-deprivation tendencies, all right around the same time. As I started examining this pattern, I realized I was depriving myself all over the place for no good reason other than, deep down, I didn't feel worthy of having a good life or having what I wanted. I'll spare you a long detour into all the historical psychological reasons that led me to habitually and unconsciously treat myself this way and instead just give you some examples that I hope will help to get you thinking about ways in which you may be unwittingly doing this to yourself. Here is just a short list, in no particular order, of some of the things I used to deprive myself of:

- Rest
- Buying anything new
- Having enough money to feel comfortable
- Pursuing my dreams
- All sorts of tasty foods
- Healthy relationships
- Healthy boundaries
- Medical care
- Vacations
- Advocating for what I needed or wanted
- Having a voice and expressing my opinion
- Having fun
- Being kind to myself in basically any way

Thankfully, I've since done a lot of work on my self-deprivation issues and have rooted out some of the main causes of that behavior. Now, when I need to go to the doctor, I remind myself that I have a great job, which I earned, with excellent health insurance, and that it's important for me to take good care of myself. Then, I go to the doctor when I'm not even on my deathbed, *and* I don't even feel guilty about it. (Gasp!)

That sounds ridiculous to me from my current vantage point, but before I woke up to the unworthiness/self-deprivation loop I was stuck in, I couldn't see what I was doing to myself or how cruel it was.

What came up for you when you read through that list? Where are you not letting yourself have what you want or need? Why do you deprive yourself in this way? These issues can go *deep*, so please be gentle with yourself as you explore and, as always, don't be afraid to reach out to a trusted friend or a mental health professional if you need support.

Appreciate Yourself

Try to see yourself from the perspective of your very best friends and closest loved ones, those who see you exactly how you want to be seen and who love you exactly how you are now. Give yourself credit for the things you *are* accomplishing and stop keeping score of all the things you haven't accomplished. Appreciate the ways in which you *do* show up for yourself and your loved ones instead of beating yourself up for not doing enough. (Preachin' to myself here.) Take some time to appreciate your uniquely beautiful body and mind and all the things you get to do with them each day!

Be Your Own Sanctuary

Belonging is a fundamental human need. It's in the same camp as safety, shelter, sleep, food, and water. In other words, no human is meant to get by without it. This includes having a sense of belonging with yourself. Without a sense of belonging with yourself, you will suffer deeply with feelings of self-abandonment, isolation, and an inability to authentically connect with others, all of which lead to a sense of hopelessness.

To practice belonging within yourself is to become your own sanctuary, the safe place you know you can always go, no matter what's happening externally, where you will be met with unconditional love, compassion, and loyalty. Without this internal safe place, we are dependent upon external conditions to provide a sense of safety and well-being for us. This would be fine if the world was made of rainbows and unicorns. Since it's not, it is incumbent upon each of us to create our own sense of inner sanctuary and safety. Here are a few tips for creating yours:

- Prioritize the things you need for your well-being *first*, before attending to the wants and needs of others, so you can actually be present and of service.
- Remind yourself that you have just as much of a right to feel good as anyone else, because you do.
- Take time to take care of your physical and mental health; to eat well, rest, play, and explore.
- Trust your gut feelings and your heart.
- Identify your most important values and act in alignment with them.
- Identify how you would like to feel inside and act in alignment with those emotions.
- Don't reject and abandon yourself in your attempts to prevent others from rejecting and abandoning you. This is a game you cannot win. No matter how many cartwheels you do, you will never please all of the people all of the time. There will always be haters. There will always be manipulators. Your work is to not be one of them, including toward yourself.
- Implement healthy boundaries that allow you to carve out this time for yourself.
- Learn to communicate directly and assertively.
- Speak up for what you want and need unapologetically and ask for help when you need help.

Those are some seriously meaty bullet points, in terms of the education and support needed to acquire the skills to be successful, but don't worry. I have done a ton of legwork for us in these areas and have created a free list of vetted educational materials and support resources that you can access by going to www.whyconnectionworks.com/bookbonuses and navigating to the Authentic Connection Book Bonuses section.

Taking good care of yourself and having your needs met is *not* selfish. It's the *only* way you can be someone who can fully show up for others. Creating the inner psychological sanctuary that allows you to prioritize taking care of yourself and having your needs met is foundational to being able to fully actualize as a human and bring your unique gifts to the world.

When you come to see yourself through the lens of unconditional love, you will come to know your inherent "worth" and that of others. You will become more capable of extending unconditional love to others. You will become a sanctuary, wherein you and those around you feel accepted, supported, loved, cherished, adored, at one, at peace; a place where you can always find ease, relief, comfort, solace, and deep replenishment. Creating this internal sanctuary will allow you to thrive within healthy relationships with others too, because you won't be so desperate for external validation that you settle for maltreatment from unhealthy partners, and you won't need to try to force or manipulate anyone into changing to please you because you will know that you can ultimately be fine on your own if you have to exit an unhealthy relationship. This is freedom! With all that subconscious pressure gone, your relationships will become more authentic, joyful, honest, fun, safe, and satisfying.

Take the Short Route

It was a painful and humbling wake-up call to realize I had almost zero capacity to enjoy myself, my amazing life, or the wonderful people in it. Finding no joy, rest, or relief when I finally arrived at the professional finish line I'd been trying to get to for so long was a real slap in the face, but it was exactly what I needed. I needed to acknowledge my deep sense of emotional deadness so I could fix it. It was time for me to wake up to the fact that no matter what I achieved, no matter how hard I pushed, no matter how much I sacrificed, none of it mattered if I couldn't enjoy it. I realized that no matter how much I gave, it would never be enough unless *I* was enough, unless the present moment was enough. I finally accepted that the grind will take as much from you as you will give it and that I didn't want to give it more of me than I already had, which was *a lot.*

Like all the practices we've discussed, becoming my own best friend and sanctuary required me to address my untended emotional wounds and diligently retrain my brain over time. As I trained myself to be a good friend to myself, every area of my life began to improve. The more I focused on appreciating myself and all the big and small gifts in my life, the more the gifts flooded in. I stopped "blocking my blessings," as they say. Not only that, but I also noticed I was actually able to pause and relax long enough to savor them. As I gave myself permission to take time for things I loved in my day-to-day life, like singing, dancing, and being in nature, the heart that I hadn't even realized had hardened over began to soften in my chest. I began to remember how good excitement feels. I began to remember how good passion feels. I finally felt the relief I'd been seeking and realized that being a good friend to myself had been the shortest route to these feelings the whole time.

We're not taught to put our relationship with ourselves first in our modern culture. We're taught to grind ourselves to a paste, stepping on each other's faces in our scramble to the top. Where has that gotten us? Depleted people have very little to share with others. They have very little capacity to care for others. They have very little bandwidth to give to their communities, or to be good stewards of their environment.

Like all friendships, your relationship with yourself will require cultivation, attention, nurturing, regular health checks, and occasionally showing up for repair, but nothing is more worthwhile. Becoming your own best friend isn't selfish. It is the first step in becoming part of the solution and the secret to a deeply fulfilling life.

7
Stop Running

True confession: this is the second time I've written this book. Most people, upon finishing their book manuscript the first time, achieving one of their lifelong dreams, would feel like they were on top of the world. When I turned in the first version of this manuscript for editing, *I* had a midlife crisis. At first, I tried reframing it as a "midlife renaissance" or "just a rough patch," but I'm just going to own it and call it what it actually was: an emotionally eviscerating, full-on, absolute crisis of a mental meltdown.

My armor first started to crack when I noticed that I had to talk myself into feeling excited that I'd finished the manuscript. After nine straight months of grinding nights and weekends to get it done alongside working my day job, I was expecting to feel more ... anything. Not only did I not feel excited, but I also actually felt completely dead inside. Completing one's biggest life dream only to feel dead inside was another giant red flag for me that some things needed to change, much like the example discussed in the previous chapter.

Right around the time I turned the first version of this manuscript in, I was scheduled to go to the Los Angeles area to participate in a two-day photography workshop. Somehow, due to a bizarre series of random events and miscommunications, I ended up in California on the wrong weekend. That was frustrating, of course, but since I was stuck there for the weekend with no workshop to attend, I did get an unexpected two-day vacation, so it was hard to complain all that much. I absolutely love the ocean, so naturally I beelined for the beach.

I couldn't even remember the last time I'd had time to myself in a nice place where there were no chores or work to do. Perhaps that had been more subconsciously on purpose than I was willing to admit. Without my cleverly devised milieu of distractions, I had nowhere to hide from myself. It was here that some real soul-searching began.

I realized that my emotional numbness was just a cover, "protecting" me from acknowledging how miserable I felt deep down. I also realized that I had an entire Numb and Avoid Toolkit. It included things like extreme overwork, chronic people-pleasing, severe control issues, and excessive alcohol use, among other toxic habits.

There, on Laguna Beach, on a perfect overcast October day, instead of continuing to run from my pain, I finally admitted the truth to myself.

I was deeply unhappy.

I had put on a happy mask to get by while enduring an extremely challenging life, in which I'd suppressed vast amounts of trauma, heartbreak, and grief.

I'd been running from this shadow for a lifetime, and if I didn't stop and deal with it, my Numb and Avoid habits were probably going to kill me sooner rather than later.

No Escape Hatch

There are things many of us will experience in this life that may require us to get professional help to work through them. If I had it my way, everyone would be assigned a therapist at birth, one who is an expert in treating trauma, because we've all experienced at least some trauma and will no doubt experience more in our lifetimes. If you don't believe me, I challenge you to consider birth, middle school, and death. Since unaddressed trauma tends to manifest into compulsive emotional avoidance behaviors, like alcohol addiction, drug addiction, shopping addictions, porn addictions, work addictions, social media addictions, and so on, these assigned therapists should probably be good at treating addiction too. Just sayin'. Most of us, if we're being honest, have some unaddressed wounds whose correlated emotions are stuffed deep down inside of ourselves somewhere, leading to struggles with unhealthy, compulsive, emotional avoidance behaviors of one form or another. The unaddressed, unmanageable emotions and the compulsive avoidance behaviors just *feed each other* and *feed each other.* We engage in the compulsive behavior to avoid uncomfortable emotions. The more we engage in the compulsive behavior, the worse we feel. The worse we feel, the more we avoid our emotions by engaging in the compulsive behavior ... you get the idea. We keep ourselves locked in these toxic loops, like a snake eating its tail.

I am not a psychiatrist or a therapist, but I do have extensive professional experience and lived experience in this arena. I feel confident positing that, if you're reading this and thinking that you are somehow the walking miracle that made it to adulthood with no baggage to unpack, you're most likely in what's called "denial." Almost no one gets out of their childhood completely unscathed, and certainly no one's getting out of adolescence, adulthood, or this *life* unscathed. Some of us hide it better than others, but sooner or later, the facade cracks and the painful emotions have to be addressed.

All of us have experienced or will experience things in our lives that are traumatic and painful. Trauma can be thought of as the emotional and psychological wounding that happens as the result of abuse, neglect, threat, witnessing violence, experiencing intense stress, or sustaining bodily injury that a person does not have the present capacity to cope with and that they feel they cannot, or could not, avoid, control, or escape.

Trauma comes in various, often intersecting, frequencies, such as an acute one-time event, a series of experiences with a beginning and an end, or an extended and chronically high-stress experience, such as discrimination, extreme poverty, living in a war zone, witnessing ongoing domestic abuse in the home, or being the child of an emotionally immature parent (or parents) with or without untreated mental health or substance use disorders or both.

Trauma can further be categorized into a variety of inter-secting types: developmental trauma, interpersonal trauma, environmental trauma, event trauma (including the loss of a loved one), body trauma, vicarious trauma, and historical or generational trauma. For our purposes here, suffice it to say that the aftereffects of experiencing trauma, if left unaddressed, may eventually require professional help for us to be able to move beyond them.

People who have been unable to address their wounding and traumatic experiences commonly develop symptoms across a spectrum, ranging anywhere from mild anxiety or depression to full blown Post-Traumatic Stress Disorder (PTSD), complex PTSD (CPTSD), other serious mental health issues, alcohol or substance use disorders, and other compulsive, self-harming emotional avoidance behaviors, such as cutting, eating disorders, and those named previously. Again, this is by no means an exhaustive list.

According to the *Diagnostic and Statistical Manual of Mental Disorders, Fifth Edition*, published by the American Psychiatric Association,

Post Traumatic Stress Disorder (PTSD) is a psychiatric disorder that may occur in people who have experienced or witnessed a traumatic event, series of events or set of circumstances. An individual may experience this as emotionally or physically harmful or life-threatening and it may affect mental, physical, social, and/or spiritual well-being. Examples include natural disasters, serious accidents, terrorist acts, war/combat, rape/ sexual assault, historical trauma, intimate partner violence and bullying. Symptoms of PTSD include intrusive thoughts and/or flashbacks and/or nightmares, avoidance of triggering reminders of the traumatic event, alterations in cognition and mood, and alterations in arousal and reactivity, such as irritability, angry outbursts, or insomnia. Many people who are exposed to a traumatic event experience symptoms similar to those described above in the days following the event. For a person to be diagnosed with PTSD, however, symptoms must last for more than a month and must cause significant distress or problems in the individual's daily functioning. Many individuals develop symptoms within three months of the trauma, but symptoms may appear later and often persist for months and sometimes years.[1]

---

1 American Psychiatric Association, "What Is Posttraumatic Stress Disorder (PTSD)?," (2022) Online. https:// www.psychiatry. org/patients-families/ptsd/what-is-ptsd

Based on experiences of those I know, I would argue that, if left unrecognized and untreated, symptoms of PTSD often last a lifetime. Similarly, I would also personally add removal of a child from their primary caregiver(s) to the examples of traumatic events included above, whether the removal is for adoption or temporary out-of-home placement.

Complex Post-Traumatic Stress Disorder (CPTSD) is a condition that can develop in people who have experienced chronic childhood trauma or chronic trauma as adults. People with CPTSD frequently experience the four typical symptoms of PTSD listed above: intrusion, avoidance, and alterations in cognition, mood, arousal, and reactivity, as well as extensive issues involving anxiety, dissociation, emotional regulation, their sense of identity, and relationships. According to the Cleveland Clinic's website article "CPTSD (Complex PTSD),"

> *Two organizations that publish professional reference books have different opinions about CPTSD. In 2019, The World Health Organization (WHO) listed CPTSD in its 11th revision of the International Classification of Diseases (ICD-11). But the American Psychiatric Association (APA), which publishes the Diagnostic and Statistical Manual of Mental Disorders (DMS-5), doesn't recognize CPTSD as a distinct condition. The DSM-5 does list a sub-type of post-traumatic stress disorder (PTSD) called dissociative PTSD that seems to encompass CPTSD symptoms.[2]*

I would go so far as to say that most, if not all, of us have experienced some form of complex trauma, because most of us have experienced being the children of parents with untreated mental health or substance use or alcohol use disorders or

---

2   Cleveland Clinic, "CPTSD (Complex PTSD)" (2023) Online.
    https:// my.clevelandclinic. org/health/diseases/24881-cptsd-complex-ptsd

grown up in otherwise dysfunctional family systems, or have endured or witnessed physical, emotional, or sexual abuse, or have lived in poverty, or have experienced discrimination and oppression, or have lived through a host of other mild to severe chronically wounding or traumatic experiences.

Regardless of any type of formal diagnosis or not, some traumatic wounds are imprinted so deeply and viscerally in the ancient, primitive parts of our brains that they prevent us from being able to make change without engaging in significant healing work first. If you've been struggling to change an unwanted emotional pattern or a harmful behavior pattern, or to make change in some area of your life, but you feel chronically stuck, like you just can't seem to make real progress no matter how hard you try, deeply embedded subconscious self-protective mechanisms that are the remnants of unaddressed wounding or trauma from your past are likely at the root of the issue. If you'd like to learn more about trauma and its effects on physical and behavioral health, please go to www.whyconnectionworks.com/bookbonuses and navigate to the Authentic Connection Book Bonuses section for a curated list of expert research and literature.

Trauma is also completely subjective and relative. No one gets to decide what is or isn't traumatic for anyone else, or the degree to which it impacts them. We also don't get to choose what is or isn't traumatic for *ourselves*. Unaddressed trauma can be retriggered in ways that are surprising and sometimes full-on debilitating. It tends to lurk around in the dark corners of our psyche, poised to jump out and leg sweep us anytime we start allowing ourselves to feel "too good," but no one needs to go through these struggles alone. Please don't make it harder on yourself and those around you by continuing to avoid and suppress your painful emotions. The compounding pressure of doing so will eventually cause you to explode like a volcano, have a complete effing meltdown, and leave horrific destruction in your wake. Think divorce, chronic illness, addiction, and other tragedies.

I could go on all day about the importance of this, but for the sake of my word count I'll just get to the point. There is *no escape hatch* from your uncomfortable emotions. Believe me, I tried them all. No one can run forever. The only way out is *through*.

The Ultimate Power Move

My aim is to hopefully save you a lot of time by encouraging you to *start* with the only truly effective option if you're seeking authentic connection with yourself, which is to do some deep personal exploration into your emotions and behaviors and what drives them. Try to take it at a slow, healthy pace and allow yourself to seek support to deal with the more challenging things you might find, if it feels right. There are more skilled professionals and more effective treatments available to us than ever before, as the research has begun to connect the dots between childhood brain development, the impacts of trauma, neuroplasticity, and behavioral health issues. If you find yourself feeling unhappy, stuck, in prolonged emotional pain, "dead inside" (AKA anhedonia), depressed, regularly anxious, chronically fearful that something bad is going to happen to you, living under a cloud of doom, engaging in harmful compulsive behaviors even though you want to stop, staying in toxic relationships, being unable to maintain healthy relationships, or frequently shaming, judging, criticizing, guilting, and blaming yourself internally, please find a professional to talk with and seek additional support. Your time is too precious to waste feeling awful, or even just "meh." You deserve to live a life that feels good.

If you have the resources and time, I highly encourage you to find a qualified treatment professional who can support you in processing your emotional challenges safely. You can search for local and online trauma-proficient therapists practicing a variety of treatment modalities through Psychology Today.com's therapists search feature.

Therapy is an investment with a return so high it's hard to put a price tag on it. That said, I also understand that our outrageously expensive privatized healthcare system in the United States makes behavioral healthcare out of reach for many individuals and families. If this is the case for you, or if you're just interested to learn more, please visit www.whyconnectionworks.com/bookbonuses and navigate to the Authentic Connection Book Bonuses section for a curated list of excellent free and low-cost media resources created by experts in the behavioral health field that may also be very helpful.

Finally, if you are ever experiencing unmanageable emotions and need someone to talk to right away, you can reach a live, trained professional anytime, day or night, by calling the 9-8-8 Suicide and Crisis Lifeline. Just dial 9-8-8 on your phone.

Bottom line: getting help is not weak, it's the ultimate power move. Most people are too scared to look at their pain, so they bury it, ignoring that it's slowly rotting them from the inside out and making them miserable. They deny themselves, the world, and everyone in it the benefits of the contributions they could make if they were willing to do the internal work necessary to release themselves from their subconscious prison of pain so they could move forward. I urge you to be brave enough to set yourself free. Start confronting whatever pain is holding you back now, so you can feel good and fully enjoy your life before you blink and it's over.

Cracking the Vault

That day on the beach, with the waves crashing hypnotically against the rocks, I made the brave choice to peer into the vault of my suppressed emotional pain with curiosity, rather than slamming the door shut on it and pretending I hadn't seen it. I discovered the deeply buried scars left over from layer upon layer of unaddressed childhood and adult relational wounds and traumas. Accepting and addressing my pain instead of continuing to suppress it was an *extremely* uncomfortable process. I feel privileged that I had good health insurance through my day job that covered a lot of behavioral health expenses, which allowed me to seek professional therapy along the way, but I did a lot of the work independently too, via books, experiential learning, self-reflection, and meditation, as many people do. I have also had the exceptional good fortune to have some very supportive and understanding friends and family members in my life, for whom I have eternal gratitude. They have made all the difference in the world on my recovery journey.

To say I feel relieved and overjoyed about the changes in my mental, emotional, and physical health would be a dramatic understatement, but I feel it's really important to say that these changes didn't happen overnight. They happened gradually over a couple of years as the result of the consistent work I did both on my own and in therapy. This critical work is not something that's ever "done" either. I still show up every day to do my own internal work because I know the massive benefits.

As you start to shine a light into the dark corners of your psyche, please take it slow, be patient with yourself, reach out for help, and always give yourself loads of compassion. Allow yourself to trust that things are unfolding just as they should be in perfect time. There is nothing to prove and no destination to arrive at. You are not broken. You are not a fixer-upper project. You are just inherently worthy, lovable you, out in the wild, learning to live a day at a time, like the rest of us. Connecting authentically with yourself is a lifelong process, and while looking deeply inside yourself might be scary at first, you will come to love and trust yourself more, and enjoy life so much more, as you get used to living fully and safely in the present, without hiding any part of you from yourself or the world.

8
End the War Within

Please enjoy this loose transcript of a conversation between two prominent and warring aspects, or "parts," of myself, facilitated by my greater Self:

Self: *"Relentless Jockey, why do you hate Drinky Poo so much?"*

Relentless Jockey: *"Are you kidding me?! Drinky Poo is making me insane! All I'm trying to do is make sure we are high-functioning. I make sure we go to work and get paid and take care of ourselves and our child so we never have to depend on anyone for money ever again. I'm just trying to get us across the finish line and Drinky Poo over there is fucking it up every night. Wasting our money. Wasting our time. Slowing us down with hangover after hangover. It's unbelievable!"*

Self: *"I understand. It is really important for us to know we can take care of ourselves and provide for our child."*

Relentless Jockey: *"Yes. It is. It's the most important thing."*

Self: *"Drinky Poo, I'm curious. Why do you drink every night, even though it's actively sabotaging the productivity that other parts of us need to feel good?"*

Drinky Poo: *"Don't I ever get to feel good?! I just want to have some fun once in a while, okay? Is that so much to ask!? All Relentless Jockey does is work and work and work. We never get to relax or have any fun unless I take over. What? Are we just going to work all day every day until we're on our deathbed and look back on our life and wish we would have let ourselves enjoy it a little? Because that's where it seems like we're headed."*

Self: *"I see. Can I ask you this, Drinky Poo? What would be even more fun than drinking, if Relentless Jockey would agree to take a little time for it? What would you really like to do that you can't do when we work all the time?"*

Drinky Poo: *"I want to be outside! All we do is sit in that suffocating office all day and we're missing everything! I want to hike and paddleboard and kayak and see some new beautiful places. We live in one of the most beautiful places on Earth and we never take advantage of it. I want to dance! We used to go out dancing. What happened to that? We used to hang out with friends. What happened to that? We used to read. We used to play music. We used to sing. What happened to those things? Now we just work all the time and Relentless Jockey is always so mean to us. It sucks."*

Self: *"You're not wrong. We haven't done any of those things we love to do in years, since the pandemic started, and work got out of control. I miss having fun too. If Relentless Jockey was willing to compromise and make time for us to have a little more fun, do you think you'd be willing to compromise and drink a little less?"*

Drinky Poo: *(Begrudgingly) "Yeah. I guess. I don't really trust Relentless Jockey, but if she's willing to try, I'm willing to try."*

Self: *"That's fair. Well, let me check in with Relentless Jockey and see if we can come to some kind of a trial agreement. How does that sound?"*

Drinky Poo: *(Folds her arms and kicks at the dirt, pouting.) "Fine."*

Self: *"Relentless Jockey, what do you think? Would you be willing to work just a little less and take some time for some recreation, so Drinky Poo might get some fun and relaxation without drinking every night?"*

Relentless Jockey: *"Well ... I don't know ... Like what? Fun makes me anxious. I'm scared that if I drop the reins everything will fall apart."*

Self: *"Well, what if we just tried a couple easy things to see how they go? If it's not okay, we can go back to business as usual. Would you be willing to try that? Perhaps we schedule a nice day hike and sign up for a dance class? No commitment, just something to try?"*

Relentless Jockey: *"Hmmm. Okay, that doesn't sound too bad. How about this? If Drinky Poo will agree to not drink on those nights and see how it goes, I'll agree to go do a couple fun things and see how it goes. I don't really trust Drinky Poo, though, honestly. I'm not too optimistic that this will work."*

Self: *"What do you think? Is that a deal you want to make, Drinky Poo? Should we try it out and see how it goes?"*

Drinky Poo: *"Deal. When do we leave?!"*

Self: *"Relentless Jockey?"*

Relentless Jockey: *"Deal." (Exasperated sigh accompanied by eye roll.)*

Self: *"All right. We have a deal. I'll block out a day for a hike, and Drinky Poo, you can help me pick the trail. Relentless Jockey, I'll make sure everything is shored up and wrapped up neatly at work before we go so hopefully you can relax and enjoy the day in nature a little too."*

Both parts murmur their skeptical consent, and I get to planning!

A Powerful Modality

Okay, if you're thinking I've lost my marbles, let me ask you to suspend judgment and hear me out for just a minute. This conversation was one of my own personal adaptations of an extremely effective and widely used therapeutic treatment modality created by Dr. Richard Schwartz called Internal Family Systems.

The general concept of Internal Family Systems is that we all have a multitude of different aspects, or "parts," within ourselves. They serve different roles but generally fall into three main categories: managers, firefighters, and exiles, which are all governed by our greater witnessing Self. Exiles are the parts of ourselves that we will do almost anything to avoid; the deep pain, grief, heartache, shame, rage, hatred, and other powerfully uncomfortable emotions that would threaten our homeostasis if we don't suppress, deny, avoid, and disown them. The other two types of parts function to basically keep us from letting exiles be seen by our conscious awareness, to keep the system "stable." These parts are referred to as managers (general protection via controlling) or firefighters (immediate emergency protection, typically via unhealthy emotional avoidance behaviors, often compulsive). The Internal Family Systems modality helps us come to understand and have appreciation for all the various parts of ourselves, and to effect system change by accepting and working with all of our parts, integrating them into one whole being, rather than living in a fragmented state, exiling and hating parts of ourselves.

I found the concepts of Internal Family Systems to be extremely helpful as a method of exploring the various aspects of my inner world to try to understand why I felt like I was always stuck in some areas of my life—always at war with myself— which had produced a tremendous amount of anxiety in me for as long as I can remember.

As you saw, I was able to identify a part of myself, Relentless Jockey, that was a manager. Upon examination, I was able to see that Relentless Jockey originally had good intentions for me. She developed as an adaptation to help me get through some really hard times, to survive and thrive, but in the last few years had started taking things a little bit to the extreme, pushing way too hard at work. It made sense. If I was always focused on work, I had no time to look more deeply inside myself at all the pain I'd buried. The problem was the overworking was causing an imbalance that was straining the whole system.

I also identified a part of myself that was a firefighter, Drinky Poo. Drinky Poo also originally had good intentions for me. Drinky Poo, under the guise of "having fun" and "relaxing" after letting my work stress reach the boiling point, was really just trying to distract me so I didn't notice the pain, grief, and rage that I'd exiled deep down inside me for so many years. Again, it made sense, but it had gone too far and was causing an imbalance that was straining the whole system.

Both Relentless Jockey and Drinky Poo ultimately shared the same goal, which was to keep me from looking at the deeply buried pain of the exiles inside me at all costs, so as not to risk me having a mental and emotional breakdown that could potentially cause the externally successful life I'd worked so hard for to fall apart.

Make Peace with Your Parts

This is what makes navigating life so tricky. The standoffs that we face tend to be within ourselves. These numerous emotional patterns and belief systems, or "parts," have developed over the course of our lives as we found ourselves having to hide parts of our authentic selves to fit into our families, communities, and society. Maybe expressing anger was unacceptable in your family, so as a small child you learned to suppress your anger rather than risk the threat of rejection or abandonment by your caregivers, whom you depended on for your survival. To your nervous system, this was a *survival-threat-level* risk. Better to stuff your authentic feeling of anger and mask it with more "acceptable" feelings and behaviors than take the risk of expressing it. These suppressed/exiled/disowned parts of ourselves do not disappear, however. They are always a part of us, and trying to lock them away as adults serves only to keep us at war within ourselves. This constant push and pull internal dynamic is why so many of us feel chronically stuck in one or more of the "big" areas of our lives, like money, relationships, and health. One part of us wants something really badly but it's up against another part of us that is screaming that it's not safe for us to have it.

Each part feels perfectly justified in pulling out all the stops to try to keep us safe from what it perceives as potential threats of annihilation. In doing so, they often go *way* overboard and end up overprotecting us, causing us to self-sabotage, paralyzing us, locking horns in opposition, and ultimately holding us back from pursuing our true desires.

If we want to put an end to this dynamic and get unstuck, we need to help the warring factions within us find some common ground. We don't want to disown these important aspects of ourselves that have been doing the best they know how to keep us alive and safe, and at the same time, we can't let them keep dominating our lives and making us miserable.

We have to find a way to integrate and approve of our exiled/disowned parts and then help them apply themselves to the greater good instead of warring against one another. First, let's talk about the *who*. Then, we'll talk about the *how*.

Below I've listed some of our most common universal emotional patterns that tend to show up as internal "parts." As you identify different aspects of yourself, you may choose to give them endearing names, such as I did with Relentless Jockey and Drinky Poo, or not. Do whatever feels right to you. As per usual, this is not an exhaustive list.

Some common internal "parts" include:

- Inner critic
- Shame
- Guilt
- Doubt
- Denial

- Excessive psychological comfort (willful obliviousness, "head in the sand")
- Scarcity mentality
- Hyper doing
- Need to control
- Worthlessness
- Hiding
- Lying
- Manipulating
- Learned helplessness
- Toxic urgency
- Paralyzing overwhelm
- People pleasing
- Chronic comparison
- Lingering self-pity
- Distraction
- Isolationism
- Emotional numbing through compulsive avoidance behaviors
- Self-harm
- Binary thinking (either/or, all/nothing)

Okay, now that we've identified some common parts we may encounter, what are we supposed to *do* with them so we can find some inner peace already? To get you started, here are some steps we can take:

1. We must decide that we *want* to end the war within. These toxic emotional loops we keep ourselves in can become addictions themselves. If an emotion such as shame strongly stimulates the survival systems in the brain/ nervous system, your body may experience a burst of

fight or flight chemicals like adrenaline and norepineph-rine, which are natural stimulants and something you may develop strong cravings for, just like you would if you ingested a stimulant regularly. Try not to judge yourself if that is the case. Just consider if this might be a compulsive loop you're in with certain emotion/thought patterns.

2. Eventually, we will find the courage to face our internal parts instead of feeding their neuroses, avoiding them, or clashing with them. When we do, we must recognize that each is an aspect of ourselves, invite them each to take their place at the table, facilitate authentic sharing, engage in compassionate listening, express heartfelt appreciation to them for doing their best to try to keep us safe all these years, and seek win/win solutions born from mutual respect and unconditional acceptance. We must find the common ground that allows us to move toward what we want together as a whole, without continuing to make *any* aspects of ourselves "bad" or "wrong." This way, rather than expending precious life energy trying to destroy these aspects of ourselves, we can join together as an internal family and form powerful, synergistic alliances for our collective greater good. Important note: Just as in the external world, often multiple rounds of peace talks will need to be held before a ceasefire or full resolution is achieved.

3. We must let these formerly shunned aspects of ourselves know that they don't need to hyper-vigilantly protect us anymore. This requires us to commit to behaving in ways that help them trust that *we got this*.

4. We must get curious and inquire as to what role they would *rather* play in our lives, one that may be more supportive of what we want. How can they put their

unique talents to good use if they want to try doing something new? Maybe they are tired and would like an honorable discharge and retirement. Maybe they still want to keep doing what they are doing until they feel safe enough to let their guard down. We must accept whatever their needs are in non-judgment. All aspects of ourselves and all our needs are valid. Our work here is not to assert our will to overpower these aspects of our authentic selves. It is to learn to love all aspects of ourselves unconditionally, express our gratitude for how they have loyally served us in the past, and create an atmosphere of trust in Self, so that they may be comfortable letting Self take over and transitioning into a healthier role within the "internal family system."

5. We must continue to hold these internal peace talks throughout the different stages of our lives, as necessary, by maturely, fairly, and diligently facilitating them with the only acceptable outcome being one that exiles and disowns *no* part of ourselves, but rather integrates all parts into a whole, and ideally healthily functioning, "internal family system." You'll know it's time to hold peace talks whenever you start to feel a strong internal sense of discord. Take that as your cue to call a cease-fire and invite everyone to the table for a round of negotiations.

Brokering Peace

Figuring out which aspects of myself were at battle with one another took some introspection and reflective writing time, but it was so incredibly worthwhile. As you saw in our conversation at the beginning of this chapter, Drinky Poo and Relentless

Jockey didn't really trust each other to hold up their end of the negotiated compromise at first. Additionally, neither of them trusted *me* to play the part of the grown-up Self and hold us all accountable for what we had committed to.

Change also wasn't one-hundred-percent smooth sailing right out of the harbor, but over time as I kept my commitment to step out of the office once in a while to get us out for some healthy fun, the contentiousness between these two aspects of myself began to lessen.

Relentless Jockey was able to start to release her death grip and see that the world wasn't going to fall apart if we went hiking for a day and didn't work into the evening so we could go to a dance class.

Drinky Poo gradually started to trust that there would be opportunities for healthy fun on a more regular basis, and my urge to drink in the evenings began to abate slowly.

Now, I want to be clear, I was also engaged in therapy and taking medication to treat alcohol use disorder, so it wasn't as if I was relying solely on doing parts work to achieve recovery. That said, I do strongly feel that using the general philosophy of the Internal Family Systems modality was absolutely *instrumental* in my ultimate success in recovery, helping me get unstuck in so many other areas of my life, and helping me find unconditional love and acceptance for myself and gain a sense of wholeness in general.

Becoming Whole

All each of us wants deep down is to be able to love and accept ourselves unconditionally, and in doing so, feel our connection to others and our oneness with all that is. We cannot love ourselves unconditionally if we continue to shun aspects of ourselves that we've deemed unacceptable. Holding these internal peace talks with our parts and honoring the commitments to ourselves that are born out of them is how we become whole. That's what makes this work so powerful.

Feeling whole and unconditionally loved is our one universal desire, at the root of all desires. Making peace with all parts of yourself is the *direct route* to having all that you truly desire most. When you do this for yourself, you will feel less anxiety and less existential loneliness, and things will more naturally fall into place in your life, both internally and externally. Of course, this was just a tiny sampling of one adaptation of this type of work. For more resources and guidance around learning to love and accept all aspects of yourself unconditionally, please go to www.whyconnectionworks.com/bookbonuses and navigate to the Authentic Connection Book Bonuses section.

9
Don't Blame the Rock

There are many natural rock-climbing areas around the mountain reservoir near my home. Sometimes when I'm out there on a hot summer's day, I like to watch the climbers work their way up the jagged red rock formations. They look so tiny from a distance.

I remember having an *Aha!* moment one bright sunny afternoon as I was floating on my paddleboard on the glittering blue water, watching the climbers inch their way up the rock faces. I wasn't feeling great emotionally that day. I was in psychological turmoil. I was feeling super burned-out from all the stress I'd been under at work. I was feeling frustrated and hurt about a thing with a friend. I was also in the habit of excessively scrolling news apps on my phone and focusing a sizable portion of my attention on all the atrocities happening in the world, which I think was less out of a sense of my personal responsibility to be an informed citizen and more just another compulsive way of avoiding personal responsibility for how I was feeling and feeding the negative emotions I was addicted to at the time.

In a nutshell, instead of deliberately *choosing* how I wanted to feel, my attitude, what I wanted to give my attention to, what I wanted to believe, and what stories I wanted to tell myself, I had been defaulting to letting external conditions and circumstances *dictate* how I felt, my attitude, what I focused on, what I believed, and the stories I told myself.

The effect? There I was, healthy, safe, free, not at work, and floating in the cool water of a beautiful mountain lake on a hot summer day, under a cloudless blue sky ... and I was miserable.

The Rock's Just Being the Rock

If you've ever rock climbed, you know that hard, jagged rocks can mess you up pretty good if you slip and fall while you're up there. Yet, climbers still go back *over and over again* to subject themselves to the skin-shredding brutality of the rock. If they show up sloppy, slip, and get hurt, they don't blame the rock. The rock's just being the rock. They understand that expecting the rock to change so they won't get hurt on it would be ridiculous. If you want to climb, you have to accept that you may occasionally get hurt. It's part of the sport.

As I considered this, I remember having the distinct thought: *Life is like the rock. Don't blame the rock. You're the one who decided to climb. You're the one who keeps banging yourself against it. The rock's just being the rock. You can keep getting angry when you get hurt if you want, but don't delude yourself about who's to blame.*

It was a solid reminder that if I wanted to not get hurt, it was *my* job to make sure I wasn't showing up out of shape, sloppy, and feeling victimized by life. I would have to put in the work to keep things tight, deliberately choosing how I wanted to feel, what attitude I wanted to have, what I wanted to give my attention to, what I wanted to believe, and what stories I wanted to tell myself. I realized that I needed to stop taking the inevitable scrapes and bruises of life so personally. Because, like the rock, life was just being life. Life wasn't *out to get me*, or anyone else for that matter. The natural challenges of life were not unique to me, nor were they personal, yet I had been taking them very personally and making myself miserable in doing so.

I realized that afternoon that it was high time I stopped feeling sorry for myself and blaming everything and everyone around me for my unhappiness. I also realized that staying in this life is a choice, and if I was choosing to stay in this life, then I didn't want to spend it dangling flaccidly from ropes at the mercy of the wind, acting helpless, and banging against the rock face over and over again, wondering why I kept getting hurt. I wanted to show up with everything I had, climb like a ninja gecko, take my bumps and scrapes along the way in stride, and be grateful to be on the rock at all.

Become Unconditional

If you insist on clinging to control over anything or anyone outside yourself as a means of trying to control how you feel, you are resisting the natural order of things and setting yourself up for a world of pain. Attempting to control external conditions so you can feel better is futile and exhausting, like a never-ending game of whack-a-mole.

You can never truly control the external world or make it completely safe, no matter how many contortions you perform. Despite how hard you may try to force people, they will rarely behave how you want them to. Time won't pause because you're tired and overwhelmed. Your body will never be all good, in every way, all at once. You can't control the endless flux of nature, politics, resources, religions, or governments.

In one way, this persistent chaos can be beneficial. The millions of things you can't control provide the perfect contrast to highlight the one immensely powerful thing you *can* control: yourself. The only way to feel safe and good in this world is to *practice* feeling safe and good *in yourself*, regardless of external conditions.

It is your work to first become aware of when you are trying to control things out of fear, whether it's overtly or through subtle, covert, perhaps even subconscious, manipulation tactics. *Really look at this*. You'll often find that when you really strip them down to their nuts and bolts, many common socially rewarded behaviors that are not suspect at first glance, such as people pleasing, martyrdom, and being busy, are actually deeply rooted, formerly adaptive, survival-based mechanisms of control and self-protection. Witnessing and remediating the manipulative ways in which you attempt to control the people and conditions around you so that you can avoid discomfort is an absolutely critical step on the journey to emotional freedom. No judgment: we've all done a few things we are not proud of because we were just doing what we were subconsciously conditioned to do to survive. I know it has been a hard thing to look at in myself at times, but the act of looking has ultimately been so beneficial. Name it to tame it, as they say.

Only when you commit to really looking at this aspect of yourself can you unravel the fear-based conditioning and become the eye of the hurricane: a calm, clear sanctuary unto yourself amidst the chaos of life; someone who's decided to feel good *despite* the chaos and despite other people's funny business; someone who's decided to make feeling good their *first priority*, no matter the external conditions, and who deliberately chooses to align their thoughts, emotions, and actions to support this. Someone who's become aware that trying to control external conditions has been controlling *them*.

As you have been learning to focus your attention deliberately, you have already been taking the first steps toward purposely choosing to feel good regardless of external conditions. Retraining the brain takes a lot of diligent practice, as you know. Learning also doesn't happen in a vacuum. Some things have to be learned in the field, by trial and error. So, try not to be too hard on yourself if you continue to have the occasional reactive moment. You will never be free from all triggers and strong, uncomfortable emotional reactions. That is not the goal. The goal is to shorten the time it takes you to return to nervous system regulation and frontal lobe functioning when you experience triggers and strong, uncomfortable emotional reactions. Try to give yourself compassion and keep faithfully returning yourself to this state of equanimity when you find you've strayed. The more you practice this, the more resilient you will become over time. As you grow your internal resilience, you will notice a corresponding increase in your sense of presence and peace, regardless of the comings and goings of the external world and the shenanigans of your fear-conditioned mind.

It really is unfortunate that we are conditioned to spend so much time trying to control external conditions "so we can be happy." Have you noticed that we never seem to fully arrive? We keep *chasing* the happiness in our environment, like the proverbial pot of gold at the end of the rainbow. We are sure we'll finally be happy when we buy a nicer car, lose twenty pounds, land the dream job, or achieve financial security. While these external conditions may bring us happiness for a little while, like a drug, just as soon as the high wears off, we'll be back out on the hunt for more.

The truth is, lasting happiness is something we have to choose to cultivate internally. It only requires that you finally accept the miraculousness of your existence, accept your inherent worthiness, and allow yourself to feel as good as you want to feel. It also requires that you let yourself let go of feeling *bad* and let those old habitual neural pathways shrivel up and die off. This is definitely not about *bypassing* uncomfortable emotions but instead about noticing when you're *wallowing* in them long past the point of productive and self-reflective processing. This happens to all of us at times, so no big deal, but when you do notice you're kind of stuck there, you can redirect your attention to the better-feeling emotions you do want to be part of your present and your future. Like all emotional patterning, it may take some time for a sense of well-being to become your habitual state, but with some consistent training, your brain and feelings of well-being will become the new neural expressway, and you won't have to work so hard at feeling good. It will be your natural state.

And What About the Others?

The people in our lives, especially the ones closest to us, are often challenging to love unconditionally because, as a function of that closeness, what they do and how they behave has the potential to cause us emotional pain. At the same time, trying to make them change to please us will only leave us chronically frustrated, and it will ultimately drive *them* away from us. People can subconsciously feel when others are trying to change them, and it is really uncomfortable to be around. This does not mean we should just roll over and put up with people's hurtful words or behaviors. Absolutely not. This entire book is about being *less* of a doormat. It means that when we choose to address someone's hurtful words or behaviors, we should take a moment to consider *why* we're addressing them. Is it to invite them to show up for relational repair by helping them understand how we were impacted and attempting to understand our own triggers more so we can ultimately deepen the safety and intimacy of our connection with each other? Or are we calling the person *out*, not *in*, lashing out or passive-aggressively shaming them in an effort to make them change so we can feel better, and thereby effectively abandoning our authentic connection with them in an attempt to control our own personal sense of safety?

The thing we have to remember is that we're all just existing here with no idea why or what any of it really means. People like to pretend they know why we're here and what it means, but in reality, we're all just surviving on this rock in space and subconsciously trying to avoid having an existential meltdown about the fact that we really don't have a clue what any of it means basically one-hundred-percent of the time. Therefore, I believe we should try to put our judgment of others in check. We would also do well to "right size" how much influence we let their opinions, moods, behaviors, and attitudes have over our own lives.

What I'm saying is, try not to let people who chronically throw shade, fearmonger, catastrophize, worry, and whine be your excuse for being out of alignment with who you want to be and how you want to feel. They don't know what they're talking about any more than you do, so you can just *decide* how you want to think and feel and *do that*. I love how speaker and author Esther Hicks expressed this sentiment. She said, "There *is* no reality that is separated from your attention to it. So, why do you let someone's attention to something that you don't want, which created some reality that you don't want, that became some 'truth' that has nothing to do with you ... why do you let that then be the thing that you think *you* should give your attention *to*? That's like saying, 'I should think the thought that I don't want to think, that makes me feel the way I don't want to feel, that will give me the manifestation that I don't want to manifest because somebody *else* did.' "

Holy mic drop, Esther.

The point I'm trying to illustrate strongly here is the most important point of this book: *you have agency*. If someone is treating you poorly, give yourself permission to have self-respect and remove yourself from their presence. If that's not an option, at the very least, remove your attention from their rotten behavior or address it directly. Whatever you do, *do not take it personally*. Other people's behavior is about what's going on inside of *them*, not a reflection of your inherent value as a human being.

I heard somewhere once that "curiosity is the antidote to judgment," and I couldn't agree more, especially when it comes to interacting with other people. Get curious about what has transpired in others' experiences that brought them to being who, what, and where they are today. Ask open-ended questions and really listen. Then ask more questions and listen some more! You'll find that people's behavior usually makes sense in the context of *their* experience and culture, even if it doesn't make sense to you. If you can, bravely share *your* story! The more we take time to hear one another's stories, the less we judge, and the more commonalities, empathy, and compassion we can find for one another.

When you're with or thinking about people you know, try to remove your attention from what irritates you about them and instead spend your time focusing on what you appreciate about them. Try to love them right where they're at, and remember that we're all part of the whole, and the person in front of you is a work in progress with a lot of potential, just as you are. Try to respect that each person has the innate capacity within them to know and do what's best for themselves. You can offer your encouragement and support, but they are on their *own* learning path, just like you are. Trying to "fix" anyone else is futile. It is part of each person's own growth experience in this life to face and overcome their own challenges by cultivating the strength and wisdom inside them. It is harmful when we rob them of their right to their formative journey by trying to fix or control them, or by doing too much and infantilizing them. This *especially* includes your partner(s) and children. Instead, try asking, "If I could support you in some way now, what might that look like?" If they ask for support and you can provide it in a healthy way for both you and them, and you *want to* provide it, then go for it! Just keep in mind: providing help we actually don't really have the capacity or desire to provide at a given time generally breeds resentment, which is unfair to both parties. If they *don't* want help, we mustn't force ourselves on them. Getting in someone's business or giving them unsolicited advice when we are not invited to sends them the disempowering and demoralizing message that we don't think they can handle the situation themselves.

Conversely, when someone feels you seeing, accepting, appreciating, and loving them unconditionally for who they are, they will blossom in your presence and they will love spending time with you, because they will feel free to be their whole, authentic self when they do. Try to give others the grace that you would like to have extended to you. Imagine if we lived in a world where we all stopped making others responsible for how we feel and decided to each claim agency over our own internal conditions instead. What could that look like?

We'll All Float On

I rolled these new realizations around in my head that afternoon as I watched the climbers. I admitted to myself that, like a rock, work stress would always be there, just minding its business, bein' work stress. Like a rock, the friend I was judging for their inconsistent communication was just existing in their natural state. They'd always been like that. I knew what to expect, so why was I all of a sudden letting it frustrate me? No one was forcing me to remain in the friendship. Ironically, the chaos of the diverse and dynamic world we live in is also dependable, in its way.

It wasn't all these issues I was fixating on that were the source of my foul feelings. I could try to blame them for hurting me, but the only thing really hurting me was my need for them to be different from their nature; my expectation that if *they* changed, then *I* would be happy. I realized that my needing things outside me to change so that I could feel better was actually the only thing standing *between* me and how I wanted to feel. I decided then and there that I didn't want to live that way anymore. I decided to stop blaming life for just being life, so I could get on with *mine*.

What a relief!

I lay back in the cool water and basked in the warm rays of the sun, feeling lighter and more free than I had in a long time.

10
Release Your Death Grip

My son was in high school when the global COVID pandemic hit. To say that he is a social guy would be a vast understatement. A real "Chatty Kathy," he has a naturally endearing way about him that generally results in his making friends wherever he goes. By early spring of his senior year, we'd been in lockdown for what felt like forever, and I could tell it was really taking a toll on him. When he started spending most of his time isolated in his room, I started to get worried about him.

One evening when we were talking, he let me in on how deeply depressed and isolated he had been feeling, and I knew things couldn't go on the way they had been. It was heartbreaking to see him hurting, but for once, instead of jumping into the fear-conditioned parenting mode of desperately trying to fix it for him, I accepted that I didn't know *at all* what to do and that any attempts at "helping" by providing every piece of unsolicited advice I could think of would probably just shut him down even more and damage our relationship, which was already undergoing some serious teenager/parent strain. I don't know why the miracle happened in that moment, but for the first time, I was able to set aside my fearful parenting ego and just be there in supportive, loving silence with him.

As I sat there, I remembered a concept I'd learned recently from a training video I'd been auditing for a work project, called *Doing Time or Doing Change?* In it, psychiatrist Dr. David Mee-Lee had discussed a concept called the "Therapeutic Alliance." A Therapeutic Alliance is formed when a therapist works to develop a genuine relationship of trust with a client, meeting the client where they're at, setting aside their own agenda in favor of finding genuine agreement *with* the client on the goals for treatment as well as the methods to achieve said goals.[3]

In this moment of parental surrender, I wondered what would happen if I released my death grip on what I wanted for my son's life and took a Therapeutic Alliance approach to parenting. What if I attempted to humbly walk *beside* him when he clearly needed accompaniment, not advice? What if I trusted that he was rightly on his own journey, that he ultimately knew what was best for himself and would find his way, and that maybe he just needed some non-judgmental, non-critical support and unconditional love during this challenging time? I took a deep breath and asked my son, "What do *you* want? What would feel better than this? If you wanted support from me right now, what would that look like?"

He answered without hesitation. He told me that he wanted to quit high school and get his GED, rather than just waiting around stagnating. He said he wanted to work full time, so he could make more money, move out, and get on with his life. He asked if I could support him by helping him figure out how to sign up for all the GED tests online so he could knock this out. His rationale was that if future employers and college

---

3 Miller, S., Mee-Lee, D., Plum, W., & Hubble, M. (n.d.). "Making Treatment Count: Client-Directed, Outcome-Informed Clinical Work with Problem Drinkers." Online. https://scottdmiller.com/wp-content/uploads/Making%20Treatment%20Count%20(Lewbow).pdf

admissions folks were ever going to be willing to sympathize with someone taking their GED and moving on with their life rather than sitting around wasting time, this pandemic would be it. I had to admit, he had a point.

But then, my fear-conditioned mind went straight to the stigma and stereotypes we perpetuate in our culture about "dropouts." I had to do some serious mental gymnastics to heave myself over that psychological roadblock, but I knew it was imperative that I set aside what I thought he needed to do with his life to "be successful" by society's rigid, hierarchical terms so I could support him in what *he* actually wanted to do with his life. I had to let go and let him define success for himself. I knew from experience how painful it was to try to live life on others' terms, and that his own intrinsic motivation was the only thing that would fuel him sustainably in the long run.

It was *not* easy to squelch my tendency to want to control everything, but I knew it was the right thing to do. I told him he had my blessing and my support to leave high school and take his GED. Silently, I promised myself that whenever I started to get panicky about it, I would not project my fears onto him. I would hide in my closet, breathe into a brown paper bag, and keep my fears to myself, where they belonged.

It's Fine. I'm Fine.

Paradoxically, experiencing everything you want is going to require you to release your death grip on controlling outcomes. You're going to have to learn to let go and go with the flow. If you just thought to yourself, "Oh, shut up, you hippy," then this chapter's for you! This chapter is also for *me*. Historically, I would have classified myself as what an old friend liked to call "a control enthusiast." Letting go of trying to control everything was a huge challenge for me.

If you can relate, don't worry—control enthusiasm is pretty common in modern culture. It took me about forty-two years on the planet to realize that it was safe to release my death grip on outcomes. Could I really just relax and trust? If I let go and relaxed, would everything fall apart?

As I started experimenting with not trying to control everything at all times, I noticed that the world didn't spin off its axis. *Things just stopped being so hard*. I noticed that the more I stopped struggling psychologically, the more things in my life just seemed to line up for me easily. *And* I got to feel good.

Wait. I could have felt like that this whole time?!

This was extremely hard for me to accept. It flew in the face of everything I'd been taught, but as it kept working more and more, I started to grow in trust. Gradually, I moved into trusting for real, like in my *core*. When that genuine deep trust clicked in, the quality of my life absolutely *transformed*. Things I'd been wanting for years, some even *decades*, began taking shape in my life with unexpected, fascinating, and delightful ease.

Often, in our attempts to control outcomes, we cram our lives so full of *doing* we have no time left for *being*, which is a terrible strategy for creating an authentic connection with ourselves and sustained happiness. Unfortunately, toxic urgency is pervasive in modern culture. It is steadily robbing us of our health, our connections, and our joy. It is so permeating and pernicious that we don't even stop to ask ourselves if the chronically high level of urgency we operate at is necessary. In most cases, it is not. I mean, we're ultimately all going to the same place anyway, right? The grave? So, what's the rush? Might there be another way? How can we learn to release our death grip? Here are a few suggestions that I hope can help:

Slow the Bleep Down

This suggestion is multifaceted.

First, I implore you to stop making a to-do list eight miles long. I can hear you arguing with me in your head right now. You could just start pumping the brakes slowly, though, instead of the scary brake-slam; letting the momentum gradually slow, so the groceries and the dog don't get thrown on the floorboards. In addition to your healthy morning and evening well-being routines, what if you made a humanly realistic, manageable to-do list of the adulting type stuff, picked the three or four things off of it that are the most critical to get done for the day, then put the big list away somewhere out of sight? What if you focused on accomplishing only those three or four things for the day? When you try this and you find that you've accomplished the three or four tasks you selected for the day, do everything in your power to resist the urge to get the list back out and feed the "Do more!" demon, unless a life or relationship or job is legitimately hanging in the balance based on whether you do another task or not. Instead, remember that the remaining tasks (and more) will be there for you to tackle tomorrow, and there will be more the day after that, and the day after that ... forever. In light of this fact, maybe it's okay to pat yourself on the back for knocking out your short and sweet daily must-do list, and then go have some actual fun *before you're dead.*

If this seems impossible right now, that's a great indicator that you've been overloading your schedule. It will get easier as you start to commit yourself to fewer and fewer unnecessary calendar obligations so you can take care of yourself more. So, the next step is to start "under-scheduling." Try to plan less into your days on purpose. Set fewer meetings. Cram in fewer appointments and errands. Say "no" to people sometimes (gasp)! I know, right? But scary as it may be, you'll be so much healthier and happier for it.

In the space that has now been freed up, you can start planning in time for relaxation and fun, just like you would any other important meetings or event. Decide how many hours of relaxation and fun you need per week or month to be the best, healthiest, happiest you and block it out unapologetically! You don't have to know exactly what you're going to do with that time when you block it out. You can figure that out as you get closer to it, but if you *don't* block it out, I guarantee it will get filled with other random B.S. that's probably neither relaxing *nor* fun. If it helps, you can use the words "nonnegotiable" or "mandatory" in your calendar. For example, you can block out small or large chunks of "nonnegotiable fun" or "mandatory relaxation" on your calendar, perhaps using a special color. When I do this, it makes me chuckle and also reminds me that I'm not allowed to cancel it. We *need* fun and relaxation. It is vital to our well-being, not to mention to enjoying the life we have. If something urgent comes up and you just *have* to encroach on a block of nonnegotiable fun or mandatory relaxation time, it's okay to bump something else on your calendar and move your nonnegotiable fun or mandatory relaxation appointment to later in the day or week, but don't you dare skip it!

Examine Your Paradigms

Releasing your death grip on outcomes is going to require rethinking the dominant paradigms you operate in. A paradigm is a cognitive framework containing the basic assumptions, ways of thinking, and methodology that are commonly accepted by a community, discipline, or group. Think of a paradigm as the unspoken, yet very real, collectively agreed upon parameters of what's socially and morally acceptable in your culture, community, social circles, and family. It defines what's within the acceptable range of normalcy in all the important areas of life like relationships, work, education, physical appearance, spirituality, and so on. These paradigms are so pervasive and hypnotizing that if we're not careful to pinch ourselves once in a while, we can easily sleepwalk through our lives, mindlessly conforming to fit in with what we're used to seeing around us without ever examining what we really want. It is *critical* that you continually examine the paradigms you're operating in to uncover which of the assumptions, ways of thinking, and methodologies that you're steeped in are actually *supporting* your empowerment and well-being, and which paradigms you need to wiggle your way out of because trying to conform to them is seriously damaging, disempowering, and life-robbing.

Ask Yourself Some Questions

When you become aware of yourself feeling super controlling and anxious around an issue, try asking yourself the following questions:

1. What is my real objective?
2. Am I trying to control the outcome of the situation to control how I or others feel, or may feel?
3. What unspoken "rules" are at play here?
4. What are the perceived "shoulds" or "shouldn'ts" in the equation?
5. Are these rules, shoulds, and shouldn'ts the objective *factual* truth? By whose standards? Do these standards make sense for *me*?

6. Might I be projecting anything onto this situation or person?
7. What things could possibly happen if I released my death grip and considered another way of being in relation to this?

Not Mine to Control

Releasing my death grip on outcomes for my son's future was *life-giving*, like releasing a pressure valve. He scheduled the four units of his GED test for a day the following month. Completing the whole test was estimated to take all day, but surprisingly he was home a few hours later. For a minute I thought he'd bailed on them, but he had actually passed them all in record time, with college-ready scores, on a couple hours of sleep, a Red Bull, and a Cinnabon. Classic.

After that, he spread his wings, went to work, and nine months later he enrolled in a community college program he was really excited about. It's been so amazing watching his confidence and belief in himself grow in the years since. Today, he is doing great in college, excelling at work, taking great care of his body, producing stunning art, enjoying his friends, spending time in nature, and is generally thriving in a way that only people with true inner confidence can.

I *shudder* to think of how differently things could have turned out had I insisted he rot in stagnation for a few more months so he could have the traditional high school graduation that I wanted for him because that's what we've been programmed to believe everyone needs to be successful.

Letting go is terrifying, but it's also so *incredibly freeing*. Like all changes of mindset, it does take time to rewire the brain and some testing of the waters to learn to trust, but with a little practice, it won't even be a question in your mind anymore. You will know in your core that you get to release your death grip on outcomes *and* receive. You'll know that true security lies not in your controlling outcomes but in your consistent alignment with your authentic self, which you can relax into any time you choose.

11
Lay Your Burdens Down

Freeing ourselves emotionally requires us to learn how to forgive ourselves, how to harvest wisdom when we're hurt by others, and how to find acceptance of the unfairness when we find ourselves the victim of very unfortunate circumstances.

None of this is easy. It can be extremely challenging, actually, but it is ultimately up to each of us to take responsibility for the way we think, the way we choose to feel, and the stories we choose to tell in the face of our pain. So often we hold ourselves captive in our pain, acting as both prisoner and our own warden. But we have to remember that what we focus on becomes magnified in our awareness. The story we tell today depicts our reality tomorrow. If we want a life that feels better, we have to tell a better story.

Too often, forgiveness is misrepresented as a one-time act you're supposed to be able to complete, and then "Poof!" like waving a magic wand, all of a sudden your hurt and anger and sadness vanish. Yeah ... um ... If you've ever tried to forgive yourself or someone else when you've been deeply hurt, you know this is what it sounds like: a fantasy.

I prefer to think of forgiveness as the continual, liberating act of accepting the reality of the past, ceasing the futile effort to change it via bitterness, regret, rumination, anger, or self-flagellation, and retraining your brain to move toward a better-feeling thought, one remembrance of hurt at a time, day after day, year after year, for the rest of your life. You can't change the past, but you *can* change your *relationship* to the past.

Forgiving Ourselves

Forgiving ourselves can be tough, but let's be honest, we've all fucked up at times. We're human. Unless you suffer from sociopathy, my guess is you were doing the best you knew how to with the information you had at the time, but still made a mistake because mistakes happen. Mistakes are also how *learning* happens. If you have since made your amends, repaired and restored things to the best of your abilities, and learned from your mistake, then it's time to forgive yourself, move forward, and do better, armed with the new knowledge that you acquired in the process. Indulging in a pity party of shame and non-self-forgiveness will only sabotage you. Taking responsibility for our impact, while at the same time recognizing that perfection is an illusion and showing shame the door, is empowering. It's our avenue to *forgive forward*, if you will, by modeling self-compassion and giving others an example that may provide them hope that they might be able to do the same for themselves in the future when they inevitably make a mistake.

Harvesting Wisdom from Hurt

People may have inflicted hurt upon you in the past but letting them rob you of your future joy as well is not only unnecessary, but it is also a squandering of your time here on

Earth. Again, I am *not* advocating for suppressing or denying or avoiding your emotions. I am advocating for each of us to take responsibility for finding our own unique balance around sufficiently processing our emotions, but not overly clinging to our pain; telling our story as needed for said processing, but not continuing to regurgitate the story of hurt so much that it comes to define us. Additionally, it can be healthy to determine what you learned from your experience that will be useful knowledge to have in the future. None of this makes the hurt someone inflicted upon you magically disappear, nor does it make it okay that they hurt you. It simply allows you to move forward with your life, letting the wound scab over and heal instead of picking at it until it becomes septic and poisons you from the inside out.

Accepting Unfair, Unfortunate Circumstances

Accepting the unfairness of unfortunate circumstances may be the hardest thing of all because often these circumstances have cost us something that was priceless and dear to our hearts. We need *somewhere* to put all that grief, rage, and the feelings of helplessness we're experiencing because of the loss.

It can be really hard to find acceptance in these situations because letting go of the hurt and anger can feel like we're being disloyal to the someone or something we loved and lost. I also know that the grief, hurt, and anger can actually feel like the last remaining connection to the someone or something we loved.

Finding acceptance for the unfairness of unfortunate circumstances is not betraying what was beloved. Finding acceptance does not mean you have to let the memory go. In your acceptance, you are simply acknowledging, "This happened. I accept that it happened. I accept that I cannot change that it happened. I choose to love myself enough to allow myself to start healing, as a way to honor what was precious to me and is now lost." Because of the nature of grief, especially when grieving for a person who has died, finding acceptance is not like flipping a light switch on or off. It cannot be forced. It can only come naturally over time as you gradually shift from the acute pain of loss into paying homage to that person's memory by focusing on all the wonderful things they brought to your life when they were in it.

Embrace Grace

Since living on Earth means there will always be new hurts on the horizon, and we know the old ones don't just magically disappear one day because we say so, we must humanely give ourselves and others grace as we learn how to practice forgiveness and acceptance.

12
Allow Your Authentic Self

Rex and I adored each other. We were unlikely companions, him in his mid-seventies and me in my mid-teens, but we were the best of friends during a very formative time of my life.

I met Rex by chance. Because there were no foreign language classes at my rural high school, and I was very interested in learning another language, I decided to save up my tips from work to take a French language and impressionist art study class at a nearby community college. What mainly drew me to the class was the trip to Paris that was included with tuition. It was an "all-ages" class, and at sixteen, I'd be allowed to go on the group tour without a parent accompanying me. I'd barely been off the farm, so it was a pretty exciting prospect for me at that age!

Rex was a retired physician in his mid-seventies, a lifelong scholar, a widower, and an art collector. He and I didn't talk much during the eight weeks of classes that preceded the trip to France, but we were cordial, as was the tone generally amongst our classmates, most of whom fell in the thirty-ish to sixty-ish age range. When the culmination trip finally came around and we got to our Parisian hotel at about 8:00am local time, after our very long travel night, something interesting happened. Everyone wanted to go take a nap. Everyone except me and Rex.

"We just got here!" I thought. *"You want to go to sleep?!"* I was incredulous. As people started to peel off from the group and head toward their rooms, Rex and I locked eyes and shared a telepathic moment. He silently conveyed to me that he was old enough to know how short his time left on this Earth was and that he didn't want to waste it *napping* while he was in *Paris*. I silently conveyed to him that I was sixteen and I could sleep when I was dead. I was ready to slam some espresso shots and go see my first foreign country!

The rest was history, as they say. We became friends because we each wanted a travel companion for that day, and what a day we had. He taught me how to navigate the metro system as we went museum hopping and sightseeing all over the city. We talked on and on about art, history, philosophy, and literature. We rode and strolled and chatted the whole day away. By the end of it, we were fast friends. We ended up spending most of that trip together being travel buddies, philosophizing our way through art museums, and chatting it up at sidewalk cafes. He was the smartest, most well-read person I'd ever met, and he recognized me for the black sheep I was, relative to the people in our conservative Midwestern culture. He was just the mentor I needed, just when I needed it.

On a cafe patio one warm evening, as we sat sipping beers and lightly discussing what I might like to do with my adult life, Rex godsmacked me with an unsolicited truth I had been blind to up until that moment. He said, "Leah, you have to stop contradicting what you want." The quiet authority in his voice stopped me mid-sentence. He let the silence between us punctuate his words. His hand was shaking with a slight tremor, characteristic of the beginning stages of the Parkinson's disease that would eventually take his life, as he slowly took a drag of his cigarette. He watched my mind working behind my eyes.

I'd been telling him about all the things I wanted to do and see in this world, but now that he was calling me out, I recognized that I had also been discussing all the associated doubts and fears in my head. Identifying all the potential barriers that might get in the way. Kowtowing to all the unspoken "rules" about how I should live my life that had been planted in my brain by others and society. I was so naturally conditioned to worry and ruminate like this that I had never even considered that there might be a choice to discuss *possibilities* without also entertaining all the doubts, fears, and what ifs. It had never before occurred to me that I might be able to give other people's "rules" and "shoulds" the finger and make my own decisions about what was true for me.

I'm certain Rex could see it on my face as the full understanding dawned on me and the implications of what he was saying to me really sunk in, because just then he leaned in toward me with the most serious look on his face. He locked eyes with me. With unmistakable gravity in his voice, he said, "Leah, *don't ever let anyone else decide how you will live your life.*"

Line Up and Let It In

This gets a little bit tricky though! It turns out, you have to actually *believe* that you can have what you desire, and that you are worthy of having it, in order to allow it into your experience. The amount of time and energy we spend throwing doubt, worry, and fear at our own desires is truly astonishing. The second we realize we want something, we immediately start the conversation with ourselves about what could go wrong along the way and why it's going to be difficult for us to reach.

We worry about what others will think of us if we go for it and start laying out all the buts, what-ifs, and potential roadblocks before we even give our desire time to hatch.

We treat doubts, fears, and what-ifs as though they are just regulars who, yeah, we don't like that much, but we feel obliged to politely entertain. For every exciting, intriguing, interesting possibility considered, we stir in a stiff shot of paralysis-inducing catastrophizing, causing ourselves to take a step backward for every step forward, and then we wonder why we feel stuck. Unsurprisingly, we cannot gain any momentum toward what we want when we are constantly waffling between the momentum of desire and the momentum of resistance. Like trying to run with one foot nailed to the floor, the two forces just cancel each other out.

The good news is that this unhelpful behavior is a product of our normal societal conditioning and we can choose to change it. Like all things brain-change, it will take diligent practice, but you can become adept at overriding the naysaying voices in your head so you can actually be *cooperative* in creating the life you want, versus being the last remaining holdout to your having it.

The most important questions here are, *Who are you authentically, and what do you truly want?* You are one with the primordial field of intelligence and infinite potential, so once you dream it up, your work is to do everything it takes to stop entertaining contradictory thoughts and get your fear-conditioned mind out of the way so you can *line up and let it in*, which means allowing yourself to feel good, calling it forth with the magnifying power of your attention, and believing that you're worthy of having it.

So, here's where the rubber meets the road. I'm going to ask you to channel the spirit of my old mentor, Rex, and engage in the following Authentic Self Mapping exercise with full candor, disregarding any doubts, fears, what-ifs, and shoulds, and really tapping into your authentic desires. I recommend finding a quiet place and giving yourself the opportunity to spend a little time in meditation getting tuned into your greater consciousness before completing it. Then, grab your journal or a pen and paper and thoughtfully answer the following questions. Alternatively, go to www.whyconnectionworks.com/bookbonuses and navigate to the Authentic Connection Book Bonuses section, where you can find a free fillable PDF version of these questions to download.

Authentic Self Mapping

How do you want to feel?

What habitual emotions will you *not* be bringing into your future?

Now that you've identified what you don't want, list the emotions you'd like to feel more of, the emotions you'd like to become the new baseline for how you typically feel.

What have you previously experienced that has given you similar emotions?

Where can you carve out time in your daily routine to spend a few minutes summoning and feeling these emotions, having an "emotional rehearsal"?

Who are you and who do you want to be?

What does the most ideal and authentic version of yourself look like? Describe in detail.

How do you carry yourself?

How do you treat yourself?

How do you interact with others?

How do you spend your time?

What is your energy like?

What are your thoughts and feelings like?

What is your appearance like?

What are the people in your life like?

What do you do for fun and relaxation?

What are your *driving values*?

Different people are driven by different values. It's important to identify our core driving values so we have them to refer to in the future at times when we're not completely sure what the best decision or course of action is. Having defined your driving values will allow you to ask yourself in these situations, "What is most in alignment with the values that I believe in most?" If you're unsure of what values drive you, search online for lists of values, and you will find many great options worth considering.

What are the overarching values that really drive your behavior or that you really want to drive your behavior moving forward?

Try to narrow it down to three to six driving values.

What are your _true desires_?

What do you most want to do, have, and experience in this life?

What are your deepest desires?

What things have you always innately known are right for you?

Nothing is off the table. This is _only_ for you. You don't have to show it to anyone else or speak of it to anyone else, but it's important to reflect on what you _really_ want. If you knew that there would only be total acceptance and you could pick anything you wanted, what would you really want to experience? As poet Mary Oliver so hauntingly asked, "Tell me, what is it you plan to do with your one wild and precious life?"

What are your _top priorities_?

While it would be lovely if we could do everything, trying to do so ultimately just dilutes our effectiveness in all areas of our lives, including the areas that are the most important to us.

Identifying your priorities will allow you to ask yourself, "Does this use of my time align with my commitment to at least one of my most important priorities?" If you find that something does not align, that doesn't mean you absolutely must never spend your time, energy, and resources on it, it just means it would benefit you to make sure that using your time, energy, and resources in that manner isn't *keeping* you from taking care of your top five priorities and doesn't conflict with them.

When you reflect on your life, what things are most important to you?

What five overarching priorities would you like to commit to serving first in your life, over all other things?

List them in hierarchical order. For example, my top five priorities in hierarchical order are as follows:

1. Tending my authentic connection to soul and self.
2. Taking excellent care of my physical, emotional, mental, and intellectual health.
3. Nurturing my relationships with my loved ones.
4. Ensuring my financial well-being while contributing to the greater good via my work.
5. Having fun.

As you can see, you can keep these priorities pretty broad. They are meant to be inclusive, not restrictive, but also to illuminate the things that are time, energy, and resource vampires in your life if left unchecked.

Fun game: Where can you combine activities to create synergy by serving multiple priorities at once? Having movie night with my family, as mentioned above, is a good example of this. I'm serving my priority to nurture my relationship with my loved ones and my priority to have some fun at the same time.

What _new beliefs_ do you need to have in place to support your living in alignment with this most authentic version of you?

Most people go through their entire lives without ever questioning the beliefs they've been programmed to have by their families, communities, and society. The truth is, because reality is subjective, not objective, beliefs are not *facts*. Beliefs are just thoughts that have been repeated so many times that they have become the easy and automatic path for the brain to take to conserve energy, like a well-worn hiking trail through the jungle. Just because they are the path of least resistance for your brain at the current moment, however, does not make them facts. Beliefs are *choices*.

Let's say you grew up in a family that taught you to believe that the harder you worked, the better and more valuable a person you were. They never spent money on anything personally enriching or fun and judged others who did so. Vacations were for lazy people and being lazy was a cardinal sin. Then, it's going to be pretty damn challenging for you, as an adult, to change your belief to be someone who values recreation, relaxation, travel, and personal development as productive and healthy uses of your time, things that are good to spend money on and allow you to be more in alignment with your authentic self, your values, your priorities, and your principles. That said, your default belief absolutely can be changed and *should* be changed if it better serves you.

Changing a belief to something that serves you may take a lot of effort and repetition at first. It makes sense, right? You'll be hacking your way through the jungle, forging a new neural pathway in your brain. The more you use that path, however, the more well-worn and easier to traverse it will become, just as the less you use the old path, the less well-worn and more overgrown it will become. It is possible to replace even the oldest and most deeply ingrained beliefs with enough effort, repetition, and a strong will to change.

Thankfully, our brains love to conserve energy by defaulting to what's called "confirmation bias," which is just a fancy way of saying that if we think a thought over and over, our brains will start to find evidence to support it. What we focus our attention on is magnified in our reality. The other hump we often have to get over is our deep fear of rejection and abandonment if we adopt a different belief system than that of our families, communities, or society. This is just something we have to examine a little more closely to unravel. Since you can never make all people happy with you at all times, wouldn't you rather be your authentic self with beliefs that serve you and have some people not be happy with you than be inauthentic and miserable and *still* inevitably have some people be unhappy with you anyway?

What thoughts do you want to put on repeat so your brain finds evidence to support them, and they become your new beliefs?

What *guiding principles* do you need in place to support your living in alignment with this most authentic version of you?

We all live by a large number of unspoken rules, norms, or principles that we are programmed to follow throughout our lives by our families, communities, and society. I'd like to suggest that, as an adult, it is incumbent upon each of us to decide for ourselves what principles will guide our individual lives and to live in accordance with them.

What are the "rules" you want to commit to living by that will serve to help you live as your favorite version of yourself and abide by your driving values?

In a world of total acceptance, what would your guiding principles be?

For example, a few of my guiding principles are:

- I am an adult and I alone get to decide how I want to live my life. Period. While I will always factor in my loved ones' needs and desires when appropriate, I ask for *permission* from nobody.
- I exercise profound respect and a sense of shared humanity when engaging with others.
- I don't allow others to treat me poorly.
- I stand up for what I believe in.
- I show up for connection and repair in my relationships and only engage in safe, healthy relationships.
- I refuse to spend my finite time on this Earth with emotionally toxic people, closed-minded people, disrespectful people, rude people, mean people, whiners, complainers, blamers, people who act victimized by life,

people who perpetuate the scarcity mentality, negative people, and people with bad attitudes.
- I live in alignment with my authentic self, true desires, driving values, top priorities, and guiding principles.
- I allow my life to be good. Really good.
- I don't buy into ridiculous superstitions like "Murphy's law," "knocking on wood," "bad things happen in threes," or "waiting for the other shoe to drop."

Do not skip this question. It is so very important for you to know your own guiding principles. Even if some of them feel lofty or out of reach when you initially write them, don't censor yourself. You will grow into them as you gain natural confidence.

What are you ready to let go of?

Without judging or shaming yourself for things you undoubtedly learned from as important lessons in the past, are there things that you've had your fill of and wish to let go of?

Are there things that no longer align with your favorite self, your driving values, your priorities, and your guiding principles?

What are you ready to change?

Are there aspects, or "parts," of yourself that would like to be thanked for their loyal service, retire their current role, and transfer into another role that better serves the whole, authentic you?

When I finally asked Relentless Jockey to hang up her whip and retire, I thanked her with deep gratitude for getting us across the proverbial finish line to a place of financial security and independence. Rather than discarding a valuable part of myself, I asked her how she *now* wanted to spend her time. She said she wanted to climb a tall mountain and sit and rest in meditation for an indeterminate amount of time. Maybe forever. I gave her my blessing. Now, I get a little smile on my face every time I sit down in meditation and fuse with that part of myself who's sitting peacefully up in that imaginary monastery in the Himalayas.

What are you ready to begin?

Now that you've done this important mapping, what are some things you think you'd like to begin doing to support the person you want to be and how you want to live?

This Is Your Life

Each time I remember Rex, gratitude washes over me for his candor and how the ripple effects of it have altered the course of my life. I didn't have a full mindset overhaul instantly in that moment, of course, but it dislodged me from my unquestioned paradigms enough to leave me at least pondering the degree of agency I held over my reality. In the two decades since Rex has passed on, the advice he gave me that sweltering hot August afternoon on a patio in Paris hasn't lost any of its potency.

Please take his advice for yourself and don't be the last thing standing between you and your happiness! Stop actively talking yourself out of having what you want. Accept that you are inherently as "worthy" and "deserving" as anyone else. Let yourself have a big, bold, beautiful life. No one else is going to give you permission. Give *yourself* permission.

13
Trust

"Daaaaaaaaamn, groceries are expensive here," I whispered under my breath. I moved on from the ten-dollar jar of peanut butter and lumbered my squeaky, wobbly wheeled shopping cart down the store aisle, feeling super self-conscious as the other shoppers cast pitiful looks at me and my loud, lame cart. I felt pitiful. Like I could barely afford to eat in Hawaii. I inwardly scolded myself for not having saved more money over the last twenty-five years. I told myself I was an idiot for thinking someone like *me* belonged in a place like *Maui*. I was overstimulated, famished, cranky, and tired. Deep Shame was taking advantage of my already spiraling attitude and trying to wrestle me to the ground.

I stopped a little farther down the aisle to stare at the shelves full of liquor. A large glass bottle of golden tequila caught my eye. My mouth watered. The thought crossed my mind, "Well, *that* would be easy ..."

I witnessed myself thinking this thought with total apathy. I guess when you're in Maui for the first time and you're miserable, that's a good sign somethin' ain't right.

I had come to Maui on a whim, needing to use up a soon-to-expire airline voucher. It was March in the Rocky

Mountains, and it had seemed like a good time to go somewhere warm. I had spent the last six months churning through endless hours of therapy, buried alive at work, and trying to stabilize in recovery. I was exhausted in every way. I was hoping that a trip to paradise would somehow magically heal my severe burnout. It was a Hail Mary pass.

Turns out, trips to Hawaii aren't really for people with modest salaries. As I started researching a trip to Maui, I quickly realized the flight voucher would *get me there*, but I couldn't actually afford a hotel room on the island. I still really wanted to go, so I did some research and opted for a more affordable option: renting a camper van and staying at a campground by the beach. "You love camping!" I told myself. "You used to camp all the time! Surely, this arrangement will be fine."

It was not fine, but learning did occur ...

I learned that living through twenty cold, dry years in the Rockies had not adequately prepared me to sweat from every pore on my body for days and nights on end. I also learned that camper van rental companies that cater to the thriftier traveler will not bat an eyelash at renting you a beat-up old minivan for the bargain price of just $180 per night. Mine had the rear seats ripped out, the bolts formerly holding the rear seats into the floor left *in*, and an inch-thick foam futon "mattress" shoved in the back on top of said bolts to sleep on. Finally, I learned that, if you love to wake up before dawn to the sound of feral roosters crowing and toddlers screaming, after sleeping crunched in a ball on a bed of U-bolts, then "econo" camping in Maui is for you.

Given that my mental health was already teetering on the brink before I traveled to Maui, you can see how being in this strange new place, feeling alone, depressed, dehydrated, sleep-deprived, overstimulated, and hypervigilant had me locking eyes with a tequila bottle and entertaining dark thoughts by the evening of day five.

On the morning of day six, I spent hours sitting in my van in a shopping center parking lot in Lahaina really laying into myself. I was ashamed of myself for how I was feeling. I was angry at Maui for not being the miracle cure for my internal misery that I wanted it to be. My mind was a swirling mess of irrational, unhelpful, and ruthlessly self-flagellating thoughts like:

"Are you serious?! Go home *early*?! Can't you even do a *vacation* right?"

"Wow, you spent all that money for nothing. Nice work. How selfish."

"You'll never be able to afford to come to Maui again. Why can't you just pull your shit together and enjoy something for once?"

"Most people would *kill* to be in Maui."

"People are going to think you're a loser if you leave Maui early."

"Way to blow your *one* amazing travel opportunity."

Trust the Process

When something feels awful, try to remember that the discomfort is serving to help you identify what you don't want more of. After you're done wanting to slap me for saying that, you will want to work on shifting your attention away from whatever it is you don't want more of by any means possible, even if only by a single degree. Rather than beating yourself up and dwelling on how bad you feel and what you don't want, see if you can find even a small sliver of gratitude for the contrast that is providing you with information and clarity. Then, work to pivot your attention to what you now know you *do* want more of, or literally anything you know you want even a fraction more than what you have now identified as something you definitely don't want.

I understand that this suggestion may sound trite because finding gratitude for the contrast with things that don't feel good is far easier said than done, but try to be compassionate toward yourself as you practice, have patience, and trust the process, even when you're feeling like crap.

Again, easier said than done, I know. That's because we've made allowing ourselves to feel good and trust the process of life ridiculously complex. Like a Rube Goldberg machine, we've overcomplicated things for so long and to such a degree that we're now farcically out of touch with how simple the original task was on its own.

The reality is, we have some choices. One choice is to trust the process of the primordial organizing force that created everything in existence, give our best good-faith effort, and let things unfold naturally. Another choice is to focus on doubt, fear, lack, and how hard everything is, and try to pound a square peg into a round hole while egomaniacally thinking that we can control things if we just pound hard enough. Speaking from direct experience, this is how one drives oneself to total burnout.

Trust Yourself

We have many senses, but only a handful are given the true credit they deserve. Emotions and intuition are at least as critical as our traditionally recognized five senses of hearing, taste, smell, sight, and touch. Cultivating awareness will help you become aware of their subtleties, allowing you to receive the important information they're trying to relay to you more clearly.

As you gain subtle awareness and live more and more in alignment with your authentic self, you will improve your ability to utilize your innate internal navigation system to your advantage. You will gradually learn to trust your intuition and emotions so much that you'll automatically check in with the information they're giving you. As things continue to get better and better for you as a result, your self-trust will grow.

If you've been a person who historically has not felt like you have trusted yourself very much, it may take some time to feel confident in doing so. That's okay. Just like the maps app on your phone, when you occasionally take a "wrong turn," you can trust your internal navigation system to course correct. Even if you end up going the "long way," you can trust that your navigation system will still ultimately take you where you need to go, via one route or another.

For instance, when I was sixteen, I knew exactly what I wanted to do with my life. I wanted to study photojournalism and work for *National Geographic*, travel the world to explore other cultures, meet interesting people, and write their stories. For a whole host of reasons, I went in a very different direction after high school. I'll spare you a long and whiny backstory because it essentially boils down to this: out of naivete, inexperience, and fear, I let other people's ideas of what I "should" do with my life usurp my own.

You could definitely say I took the "long way." I won't lie and say that I was always glowing with trust for myself or the process along the way. In fact, I felt terrifyingly uncertain of where I was and where I was going most of the time. In retrospect, getting lost on the back roads and finding my way anyway is what taught me how to trust myself and trust the process of life. Here I am twenty-some years later, deeply engaged in both writing and photography, having recently returned from a very fun and redeeming trip to Oahu, and with more travel on the horizon. I get to work with a wide variety of people, and I love to hear their unique stories and transfer the lessons I learn from them to my work. Even though I took the "scenic route," I can see now that my internal navigation system was always working in the background, pointing me to where I knew I ultimately wanted to go, and that life was unfolding for me just as I needed it to for my personal growth. If given the choice to go back and do it all over again, even with all the detours and flat tires, I would still choose the "long way" every time.

You Get What You Need

Maui didn't turn out to be exactly what I *wanted* it to be, but it *did* turn out to be exactly what I needed it to be.

After some very uncomfortable but very necessary self-reflection, I had a breakthrough. I realized that I couldn't recall a time in my life when I had allowed myself to fully trust myself. The burnout I was experiencing was real, but it wasn't the cause of my issues; it was a *symptom*. The burnout was from trying desperately to run away from the accumulation of decades of suppressed emotional pain and exhaustion. For years now, this unresolved pain had been boiling up within me, like pressurized lava threatening to blow the top off the volcano at any moment. I realized if I wanted to start to heal, I would have to start trusting myself and developing a secure and safe relationship with myself.

From where I sat, I saw myself having two options to decide between. I could carry on with my original travel plans for my last few days on the island, which entailed my driving the rickety old minivan up the Road to Hana alone. The Road to Hana sounded beautiful by all accounts. Everybody said it was the "must see" of Maui. In reality, I knew that in my extremely frayed state, I would be feeling super anxious driving it, staring at the back of someone else's bumper for four hours, eek-ing my way around hairpin turn after hairpin turn, praying the van didn't break down. I would then be camping alone at a primitive campground in the national park that was many, many miles past the town of Hana. With the portable car battery charger I had, it was looking like I could either make sure my cell phone was charged *or* reserve enough charge to jumpstart the van if its battery died on me. I would spend three long nights on a bed of bolts feeling lonely, cold, vulnerable, and isolated, in an unfamiliar place, cell service-less and emotionally depleted, all for the sake of not disappointing the small handful of people who had told me, "If you're in Maui, you *have to* drive the Road to Hana." I would also then have to jump on a plane for a twelve-hour trip home as soon as I got back from the east side of the island and slam back into work the very next morning.

My other option was to try to change my flight and go home three days early. Initially, I had a lot of shame when I started seriously entertaining the idea of going home prematurely. Again, my inner critic wouldn't let me live it down that I couldn't "do Maui" correctly, or that I'd be a big fat loser for being this close and not driving the Road to Hana. It told me I was wimping out. It was also fearmongering, telling me that this was my only chance ever to drive the Road to Hana and I was wasting it.

I decided to check in with my true feelings about these two options without judging them. I just sat with myself and listened.

When I thought about the Road to Hana, cold camping, and then having to dive straight back into mountains of work upon returning home, it sounded grueling. When I thought about leaving a few days early and using those few extra days at home as a staycation to rest and get my head back together before returning to work, it felt relieving. It would seem to be a pretty straightforward decision, except it wasn't. I wrestled with myself for *hours* before finally giving myself permission to choose what truly felt best and safest for *me*, in spite of all the "shoulds" of others rolling around in my psyche.

I called the airline the next morning. They were able to change my flight at no cost and get me on a flight leaving early the following day. I felt an enormous wave of relief. Then something unexpected happened. I felt *proud* of myself. Like, legitimately proud of myself. I was proud of myself for making a healthy decision, in *alignment* with my authentic self, in the face of intense internal resistance, shame, and the fear of what others might think. I had the distinct knowledge that I'd planted a little seed of self-trust that would, in time, grow into a great big sturdy *oak* of self-trust.

I still had a day to kill in Maui, and I was now feeling the euphoric relief one feels when one has made a self-loving decision after wrestling with extreme angst. I decided to go on a whale watching tour. We saw at least a dozen whales that afternoon. A friggin' *baby* humpback breached right in front of our boat. It was incredible.

For my last evening in Maui, I went back to a beautiful tucked-away beach I'd found earlier that week. It was a gorgeous forever strip of white sand meeting blue water. There were only a handful of other people there. I strolled along the beach with my feet in the waves for hours, feeling a deep sense of ease. Then, the sun began to set and the entire sky lit up in brilliant pinks and oranges. I stopped and stood there, motionless, rapt, watching the sunset's reflection set the vast ocean on fire, the waves gently lapping at my toes. I was lost in the moment, suspended in time, completely at one with myself and the universe. It was the most beautiful sunset I've ever seen. The image of it is permanently burned into my mind and heart as an irrefutable affirmation that I could, *and should*, trust myself to know what's right for me.

When the sky finally went dark and I realized it was time to leave, I had to wipe away a waterfall of tears that I hadn't even noticed streaming down my cheeks. There aren't words to adequately describe the deep, soul-cleansing peace I felt. I knew things were going to be different for me now. I knew *I* was different.

Give Yourself Permission

Trust is giving yourself permission to say yes to *all* of life, knowing that you will be okay because you know that no matter what, *you* have your back and you are inseparably part of all that is. It is allowing yourself to be fully present in this dynamic process of life as the most authentic version of yourself. It is to welcome the fullest expression of your life bravely, in full knowledge of what that entails: giving *and* receiving, pleasure *and* pain, love *and* loss, joy *and* sorrow. It's agreeing to bear all of it, in its full magnitude, without sacrificing your innocence. It is the knowledge that to *fully* show up for this beautifully unfolding experience is to trust yourself even when it's scary, to say yes to what your heart desires even though you could lose it, to love with your whole being even though it may hurt, to laugh until you cry, to cry until you laugh, *and to know that you wouldn't have it any other way.*

Conclusion

Thank you for taking this journey with me and engaging in deep exploration of the inner landscapes that shape our relationships with our authentic selves. Not everyone is brave enough to look inside and get really real with themselves, but you did. I commend you for doing so and hope that you have found the journey rewarding.

Through the practices in this book, we examined how our relationships with ourselves have been governed largely by family, community, and societal expectations, our lack of being in command of our attention, the residual reactivity of unaddressed trauma, and self-imposed limitations.

Cultivating awareness allows us to become the witness of ourselves as part of the whole of existence as well as the witness of our individual consciousness in our physical body. Being able to step back and see the bigger picture helps us remember to not take the perceived slights of life so seriously or so personally. It teaches us that we do not have to be at the mercy of our fear-conditioned minds and emotions.

Meditation, as a foundational practice, allows us to cultivate awareness, become present in the now, and witness our thoughts without judgment or attachment. It helps us learn to observe and recognize our mind's patterns so we can put some space between having a thought and responding to it, which allows us to proactively choose responses that serve us. In meditation, we are able to find the deep stillness that we intuitively crave. It is in this deep stillness that we are able to hear the whisperings of our hearts, bodies, and inner wisdom.

Reflective writing, or journaling, is a great companion practice for meditation because it provides an important outlet for our inner dialogue. This can help us find greater clarity, solidify powerful insights, and come to better understand our thought patterns, emotional patterns, intrinsic motivations, and behaviors.

We befriended our bodies and ourselves. We learned about the importance of physical and emotional self-regulation in helping us do so. Practicing physical and emotional self-regulation puts us, our prefrontal cortex, back in the driver's seat so we can exert control over how we respond to stimuli rather than acting on every whim of our sympathetic nervous system's knee-jerk survival responses. This allows us to practice self-compassion, which can be a powerful antidote to our standard self-trash-talking. Self-compassion invites us to treat ourselves with the kindness and empathy we would show a cherished loved one, so we can come to trust that we will not emotionally reject or abandon ourselves when the going gets tough. Taking good care of our bodies through basic practices like getting adequate rest, exercise, nutrition, and hydration sends us the same messages about ourselves: we are valuable enough to treat well. Befriending our bodies in these ways also promotes improved physical, mental, and emotional health.

Taking a good look at ourselves and addressing the hurts we have endured throughout our lives is a courageous act of reclaiming our power to shape our own story. By acknowledging and processing our wounds, we liberate ourselves from their grip and pave the way for healing and change. Seeking the guidance of trained behavioral health professionals can provide invaluable support on this challenging leg of the journey.

Making peace with the various aspects of ourselves is a practice that can lead us to a profoundly healing sense of wholeness, harmony, and peace. Embracing and accepting the myriad parts of ourselves allows us to end the war within and live as a more integrated, and thereby more authentic, expression of ourselves.

Taking responsibility for our thoughts, feelings, emotions, and behaviors allows us to reclaim our agency and create meaningful, lasting change in our lives. By acknowledging that we are simply co-creators of our reality, in partnership with the infinite field of primordial intelligence, we can release the neurotic idea that we can and should control everything. Releasing our death grip on outcomes allows us to develop a more relaxed, fluid, realistic, and comfortable relationship with life, so we can delight in its dynamic and synchronistic unfolding. We discussed other things it would benefit us to let go of as well, such as guilt, anger, bitterness, hatred, shame, resentment, and blame. Laying down these burdens doesn't let anyone off the hook for wrongs they've inflicted upon us, it simply relieves us of carrying the weight so we can devote our energy to healing and flourishing.

Allowing our authentic selves to exist in the world involved first identifying the core version of ourselves that we've been dying to fully express. Then we identified our driving values, our top priorities, and our guiding principles, which helped us start aligning our thoughts, words, feelings, and behaviors with them. It is through this alignment that we can continue to cultivate a sense of authenticity, joy, aliveness, and purpose.

Finally, we explored practices for learning how to trust ourselves and trust the process of life. Learning how to trust allows us to return to the state of innocence we came into this world with, in which we naturally trusted ourselves and the process of life. That state of innocence feels incredible because it is the purest expression of our true, authentic, whole selves. Trusting ourselves is, then, the ultimate self-validation. Trusting the process of life is the ultimate surrender, removing any resistance that would keep us from the ecstasy of feeling our oneness with the beautiful eternal unfolding of existence.

Ultimately, the journey of authentic connection is one of liberation—an inner pilgrimage leading us home to ourselves. May we always remember that the destination is not a place but a state of being. Our embodiment of infinite possibility, presence, wisdom, and love. The reverent act of allowing ourselves to fully actualize and share our gifts and blessings with the world.

In closing, I would like to extend my heartfelt thanks to you for the valuable time and energy you dedicated to reading this book. I sincerely hope that something in these pages inspired you and that you are enjoying applying the practices we've explored to your own life. If so, I'd love to hear all about it. You can connect with me by emailing leah@whyconnectionworks.com. I welcome any questions you may have or constructive feedback you wish to share. Finally, don't forget to go check out the powerful free tools and resources available in your book bonuses at www.whyconnectionworks.com/bookbonuses.

In gratitude,
Leah Marie Price

Final Author's Note
The Hill I'm Willing to Die On

Based on my personal and professional experience, I believe that behavioral health, defined as "an individual's mental and emotional well-being and actions that affect an individual's overall wellness,"[4] is the foundation of *all* health.

According to SAMHSA's 2022 National Survey on Drug Use and Health Data, "48.7 million people aged 12 or older (or 17.3%) had a substance use disorder (SUD) in the past year, including 29.5 million who had an alcohol use disorder (AUD), 27.2 million who had a drug use disorder (DUD), and 8.0 million people who had both an AUD and a DUD. In 2022, almost 1 in 4 adults aged 18 or older had any mental illness (AMI) in the past year (59.3 million or 23.1%)."[5]

These untreated substance use, alcohol use, and other compulsive behavioral health disorders and mental health issues have disastrous health outcomes for individuals, families, and society. Therefore, it stands to reason that expanding access to behavioral healthcare, especially in a preventative sense and

---

4   About the BHA | Behavioral Health Administration. (n.d.). Bha.colorado.gov. (2024) Online. https://bha.colorado.gov/about-us
5   SAMHSA. (2023, November 13). *HHS, SAMHSA Release 2022 National Survey on Drug Use and Health Data*. www.samhsa.gov. https://www.samhsa.gov/newsroom/press-announcements/20231113/hhs-samhsa-release-2022-nsduh-data

in conjunction with a broad educational and destigmatization campaign, has the strong potential to *significantly lower all types of healthcare costs* while significantly *improving* our collective quality of life and the overall health of our communities. We must stop criminalizing behavioral health disorders and start *treating* individuals who suffer from them, so we can end generational cycles of unaddressed behavioral health needs. We can then have safer and healthier communities without unnecessary incarceration, which is inhumane, extremely expensive, and actually leads to significantly *worse* health and community safety outcomes over time.

In my many years of professional experience working at the confluence of behavioral healthcare and the criminal legal system, it has become apparent that newly trained therapists and clinical social workers largely only stay employed in agencies that accept Medicaid and Medicare, or the Veterans Administration (VA), long enough to complete their required supervision hours for licensure (typically two years or less), before they go into private practice or a small group practice where they can make more money and in which they typically do *not* take Medicaid or Medicare. I do not fault them for this, given the way our system is set up. They have to do what they have to do to be able to earn a living that will allow them to pay back their mountain of student loan debt somehow too, right? However, this reality leads to a shortage of treatment providers in general, and an *extreme* shortage of the type of highly experienced treatment providers who would be most qualified to serve our most vulnerable, high-need community members. This lack of accessibility to appropriate behavioral healthcare for this population, and for all of us, has dramatic negative ripple effects on generations of our families, communities, and society at large.

It is my position that individuals who are willing to train to become therapists or licensed clinical social workers, and who work for behavioral health treatment agencies who accept Medicaid and Medicare, or for the VA, should be made eligible for the Public Employee Student Loan Forgiveness program or something similar that offers student loan forgiveness to those who serve in these understaffed agencies for ten years. This would ultimately serve to address the problem from a few angles. First, it would keep many treatment providers working in behavioral healthcare agencies that accept Medicaid and Medicare, and in the VA, much longer, as they would be accruing years toward student loan forgiveness. This would naturally expand the pool of treatment providers by keeping them in these treatment agencies and attract more students to the fields of therapy and clinical social work. It would also ensure that more therapists and clinical social workers with experience and expertise were more available to our most vulnerable and high-need community members via treatment agencies that accept Medicaid and Medicare, and the VA. In time, this expansion of access to treatment providers would likely serve to bring behavioral healthcare costs down overall. Finally, the expansion of education and access to *preventative* behavioral healthcare would ultimately serve to stem the flow upstream, getting people needed care much sooner, preventing many of them from developing more severe behavioral health issues that tend to lead to much more costly individual, family, community, and societal health impacts.

My hope is that someone reading this will *be* someone, or will *know* someone, who has the economic insight or political influence to move research on this potential solution forward in a meaningful way, so that more individuals, families, and communities may be able to escape the devastating impacts of untreated substance use, alcohol use, and mental health disorders.

Behavioral healthcare is *the foundation* of healthcare and a basic human right that should be available to everyone, not just a privileged few.

Acknowledgments

Special thanks to my family and friends for believing in me, inspiring me, and continually encouraging me throughout this process. Your support has meant the world to me. I am so grateful to have you in my life.

Special thanks to Matt, Rob, Bob, and the rest of the team at Best Seller Publishing for your expertise, vision, and unparalleled care every step of the way.

www.ingramcontent.com/pod-product-compliance
Lightning Source LLC
Chambersburg PA
CBHW051313120626
46547CB00015B/2213